EMOTIONAL INTELLIGENCE TO EMPOWER WOMEN

MASTER YOUR EMOTIONS, BUILD YOUR STRENGTH, CHANGE YOUR LIFE

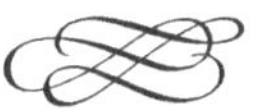

AKARI YIN

To my beloved grandparents,

Your courage in seeking a new life and your wisdom in preserving our traditions have been my greatest inspirations. Thank you for teaching me the balance of harmony and progress and for instilling in me the strength to bridge worlds. This book is a testament to your enduring love, resilience, and the rich legacy you have gifted me.

CONTENTS

INTRODUCTION

Hello, my friends!

Welcome to a personal, powerful, and transformative journey. This journey is about you and understanding your emotions, mental health, and, ultimately, your incredible capacity for growth and change.

We will explore something that lives deep within us yet often goes unacknowledged: our emotional intelligence. Emotional intelligence isn't just about being able to identify and manage our own emotions. It's about understanding the feelings of those around us, which may influence our relationships, decisions, and mental health.

Have you ever felt like your emotions are running the show? Or perhaps you've felt disconnected from them, unsure how to bridge the gap? This is where emotional intelligence comes into play. It's about learning to see our emotions as tools, not obstacles, as guides that lead us toward a healthier, more balanced state of mind.

Now, you might wonder, "What does emotional intelligence have to do with mental health?" That's a great question and one we're going to explore. Our mental health doesn't exist in a vacuum; many factors influence it, and emotional intelligence is key. Enhancing our emotional intelligence can build resilience, foster healthier relationships, and cultivate a more positive mindset—all of which contribute to our overall mental well-being.

I've written this book to aid you on your journey to empowerment. It's not a set of rigid rules or a one-size-fits-all blueprint but a guidebook filled with insights, exercises, and everyday scenarios to help you navigate your emotional landscape more quickly and confidently.

We'll approach this journey with empathy and understanding. We all have different experiences, strengths, and weaknesses. Additionally, this book is designed to meet you where you are, providing specific recommendations that align with your unique circumstances.

Remember this: You are not alone on this journey. Like you, I've faced challenges in understanding the correlation between emotional intelligence and mental health. My passion for this topic stems from my upbringing, personal experiences, and desire to help women feel more understood, capable, and empowered.

So, are you ready to begin? Let's take this journey together. Your path to understanding, growth, and empowerment starts here.

THE ESSENCE OF EMOTIONAL INTELLIGENCE

Between stimulus and response, there is a space. In that space lies our freedom and power to choose our response. In our response lies our growth and freedom.

—VIKTOR E. FRANKL

DID you know that emotional intelligence is listed on the World Economic Forum's list of the top skills that employees will need to possess to thrive in the workplace of the future? It's true. Emotional intelligence is no longer simply "nice to have" but a critical skill necessary for personal and professional success. But what exactly is emotional intelligence?

Emotional intelligence is the ability to positively understand, use, and manage our emotions to relieve stress, communicate effectively, empathize with others, overcome challenges, and diffuse conflict. Emotional intelligence involves five key components: Self-Awareness, Self-Regulation, Motivation, Empathy, and Social Skills.

Self-Awareness

Self-awareness is the first step towards emotional intelligence. It's like turning on a light in a previously dark room, illuminating previously hidden areas. Self-awareness is about recognizing our emotions and how they affect our thoughts and behavior. It's knowing our strengths and weaknesses and understanding how we come across to others.

Think about the last time you felt frustrated or upset. Were you aware of these emotions as they occurred, or did you only recognize them after the fact? By improving our self-awareness, we can acknowledge our feelings as they arise, allowing us to navigate our responses better.

Self-Regulation

Self-regulation is the act of controlling our emotions and impulses rather than being ruled by them. It's about expressing our emotions appropriately and effectively. You know that feeling when you're about to burst with anger but somehow manage to keep your cool? That's self-regulation in action.

Let's say you're in a heated discussion with a coworker. You feel your anger rising, but instead of lashing out, you take a deep breath, calmly express your feelings, and turn the argument into a constructive conversation. This is the power of self-regulation.

Motivation

Motivation in the context of emotional intelligence doesn't just refer to our drive to achieve our goals. It's about having a positive outlook, a strong desire to succeed, and persisting through obstacles. Emotionally intelligent people are self-motivated, flexible, and resilient.

Imagine you're working on a challenging project, pushing your skills to the limit. Instead of getting discouraged by the difficulties, you view them as opportunities for growth. You stay motivated, remain focused on your goal, and persist until you succeed. This kind of intrinsic motivation is a vital component of emotional intelligence.

Empathy

Empathy is the ability to understand and share the feelings of others. It's about more than just being able to recognize others' emotional states; it's about understanding their emotions, needs, and concerns from their perspective.

Consider a girlfriend who is going through a tough time. Empathy means you can understand her emotions and respond in a way that shows you care. You can put yourself in her shoes, offering comfort and understanding without judgment.

Social Skills

Social skills are crucial for building and maintaining healthy personal and professional relationships. These skills include effective communication, conflict management, leadership, and teamwork.

Think back to when you led a team project, or hypothetically, imagine you're the point person on one. You ensure everyone's views are heard, conflicts are resolved amicably, and the team remains motivated throughout the project. You communicate effectively and foster a positive environment where everyone feels valued. These are social skills, a crucial element of emotional intelligence.

As we navigate life, we constantly interact with others, face challenges, and experience many emotions. By understanding and applying the five components of emotional intelligence, we're better equipped to handle whatever life throws our way. Emotional intelligence is not just about emotions; it's about using our understanding of emotions to live a happier, healthier, and more fulfilling life.

In the following chapters, we'll explore these components more profoundly and provide practical strategies to enhance emotional intelligence and improve mental health. So, let's get started!

THE ROLE OF EMOTIONAL INTELLIGENCE IN LIFE

Emotional intelligence isn't just a trendy buzzword. It's a fundamental aspect of our lives, influencing our relationships, work, mental health, and personal growth. Let's look at how this plays out in everyday life.

Enhancing Personal Relationships

Relationships are the heart of our lives. They bring us joy, support, and companionship. However, they also bring challenges, disagreements, and misunderstandings. Emotional intelligence can help us navigate these waters more effectively.

Understanding and managing our emotions can help us respond to conflicts more constructively. When we're aware of our emotions, we can express our feelings and needs clearly and directly, reducing misunderstandings. When we can regulate our emotions, we're less likely to say or do something in the heat of the moment that we might regret later.

Empathy, another crucial aspect of emotional intelligence, enables us to understand the emotions and perspectives of others, fostering deeper connections and mutual respect. And let's not forget our social skills, which allow us to communicate effectively, manage conflicts, and build strong, fulfilling relationships.

Improving Professional Success

Emotional intelligence is just as vital in the workplace, if not more so. It can help you navigate the complexities of workplace dynamics, foster productive relationships, and lead others more effectively.

Picture yourself in a corporate meeting where tensions are running high. When you're emotionally intelligent, you can pick up on the subtle emotional cues in the room. You'll understand that your colleague isn't just being difficult; she's stressed about an upcoming deadline. You'll know your boss isn't just being critical; she's dealing with pressure from higher-ups.

This understanding can guide your actions and responses, helping you navigate the situation more effectively. For example, you might offer to help your stressed colleague or find a way to alleviate some of your boss's pressure. This makes the workplace more harmonious and positions you as a valuable, empathetic team member.

Boosting Mental Health

Emotional intelligence and mental health are deeply interconnected. By managing our emotions effectively, we can reduce stress, overcome challenges, and maintain a positive outlook, all contributing to better mental health.

Consider the impact of negative emotions. Unresolved anger, for example, can lead to stress, relationship problems, and even health issues. But if we're emotionally intelligent, we'll recognize the anger early on. We'll understand what triggered it and how it's affecting us. Most importantly, we'll learn how to express and manage this anger in a healthy, constructive manner.

Emotional intelligence can help us deal with anxiety, sadness, and other challenging emotions. It can even help us recognize the early signs of more serious mental health issues, prompting us to seek help when needed.

Nurturing Self-Growth

Last but certainly not least, emotional intelligence plays a crucial role in our personal growth. As we improve our emotional intelligence, we better manage our emotions, deal with challenges, and grow as individuals.

Emotional intelligence helps us understand ourselves on a deeper level. It illuminates our strengths and weaknesses, triggers and patterns, and needs and desires. This self-awareness is the foundation for personal growth.

With emotional intelligence, we can set meaningful goals that align with our values. We can be more resilient in the face of adversity and more adaptable in the face of change. We can be more authentic and more fulfilled in our relationships. In other words, emotional intelligence is not just about dealing with emotions; it's about living a richer, fuller, and more meaningful life.

So, as you can see, emotional intelligence doesn't just affect one area of our lives. It affects every area of our lives. Emotional intelligence is crucial to our overall well-being and success, from our relationships to work, mental health, and personal growth. And the best part? Emotional intelligence is not a fixed trait. It's a skill that we can develop and improve over time. We can become more emotionally intelligent with practice, patience, and perseverance. And as we do, we'll find that every aspect of our lives begins to change for the better.

EMOTIONAL INTELLIGENCE VS. IQ: THE KEY DIFFERENCES

While we're on emotional intelligence, it's essential to discuss its relationship with another well-known concept: Intelligence Quotient, or IQ. Contrary to popular belief, IQ and emotional intelligence are not two sides of the same coin. They represent different aspects of our cognitive abilities and play distinct roles in our lives.

Emotional Intelligence: Understanding and Managing Emotions

As we've discussed, emotional intelligence is the ability to perceive, understand, and manage one's and others' emotions. It allows us to navigate social complexities, make informed decisions, and maintain mental well-being.

For instance, if you're emotionally intelligent, you're likely good at recognizing when you're feeling stressed and taking steps to manage that stress. You can empathize with a friend or acquaintance going through a tough time and offer them the support they need. In a heated argument, you can keep calm, listen to the other person's perspective, and find a resolution without losing control of your emotions.

IQ: Cognitive Abilities and Knowledge Processing

IQ, on the other hand, is a measure of your cognitive abilities. It's about logical reasoning, verbal skills, mathematical aptitude, and problem-solving abilities. It's the score you'd get on a standardized intelligence test, and it's often associated with academic success.

For example, if you have a high IQ, you're probably good at logical reasoning tasks like puzzles and problem-solving exercises. You might excel in academic subjects that require analytical thinking, like math and science. You can learn quickly, remember information, and apply that knowledge in different contexts.

The Interplay and Balance between EQ and IQ

Now, you might wonder - which is more critical, EQ or IQ? The answer isn't as straightforward as you might think.

IQ and EQ play different roles in our lives and can complement each other. A high IQ can help you excel in school and work, especially in fields that require analytical thinking and problem-solving. However, you might struggle with social interactions, managing emotions, and maintaining mental well-being without a high EQ.

Envision a brilliant scientist with a high IQ but low EQ. They might make groundbreaking discoveries in their field but struggle with collaborative projects, stress management, and interpersonal relationships. On the other hand, a person with a high EQ but an average IQ might not be a scientific genius. Still, they'll likely have strong relationships, good mental health, and the ability to navigate life's challenges with grace and resilience.

While both IQ and EQ are important, they serve different purposes. IQ is a critical component of cognitive intelligence, while EQ is vital for emotional and social intelligence. One isn't superior to the other; they balance each other equally.

Ultimately, the most successful and fulfilled individuals have often learned to harness their IQ and EQ. They can solve complex problems, develop innovative ideas, understand and manage their emotions, maintain strong relationships, and handle stress effectively.

A high IQ without EQ is like a car with a powerful engine but no steering wheel. You can go fast but can't control where you're going. On the other hand, having a high EQ without a good IQ is like being a car with a perfect steering system but no engine. You can't move forward, no matter how well you can steer.

The key lies in balance. By understanding and developing our IQ and EQ, we can drive our lives in the direction we want, at the speed we want, and with the control we need. This, ultimately, leads to a fulfilling, successful, and balanced life.

While IQ and EQ are different, they're both essential puzzle pieces. They complement each other, and together, they paint a complete picture of our cognitive abilities. Understanding and nurturing our IQ and EQ allows us to live a richer, more balanced, and more fulfilling life.

THE NEUROSCIENCE BEHIND EMOTIONAL INTELLIGENCE

Understanding the neuroscience that underlies emotional intelligence is helpful for fully comprehending it. The brain, our command center, is pivotal in our emotional responses and decision-making processes. Let's explore the fascinating interplay between two key players in our brains: the amygdala and the prefrontal cortex.

The Amygdala: Emotional Processing Center

The amygdala (ah-MIG-dah-la), named after its almond-like shape, serves as our emotional processing center. This small structure deep within our brain is constantly on the lookout, ready to respond to perceived threats. It is like a diligent guard dog, always alert and prepared to protect us.

When we experience an emotional event, the amygdala springs into action. It assesses the situation, decides whether it's threatening, and triggers an emotional response. If it senses danger, it can initiate a fight, flight, or freeze response, preparing our bodies to deal with the threat.

Let's imagine you're walking down a dark alley late at night. Suddenly, you hear a rustling sound behind you. Your amygdala kicks in, flooding your body with adrenaline and preparing you to either confront the potential threat or swiftly exit. This automatic, rapid-fire response from the amygdala is essential for our survival.

The Prefrontal Cortex: Rational Decision-Making

While the amygdala is our emotional powerhouse, the prefrontal cortex is our rational decision-maker. Located at the front of the brain, the prefrontal cortex is responsible for higher cognitive functions like planning, decision-making, and moderating social behavior.

The prefrontal cortex allows us to think before we act, consider the consequences of our actions, and make rational decisions. It's like a wise mentor, guiding us to make decisions that align with our long-term goals and values.

Think of a time when you were at a gathering, and someone made a comment that rubbed you the wrong way. Your initial emotional response, triggered by the amygdala, might be to snap back with a retort. However, your prefrontal cortex steps in, reminding you of the potential social consequences of such an action and guiding you to respond more calmly and diplomatically.

The Connection between the Amygdala and Prefrontal Cortex

You might be wondering how these two distinct brain regions work together. How do the emotional amygdala and the rational prefrontal cortex interact to create our emotional responses?

The connection between the amygdala and the prefrontal cortex is a bit like a seesaw. When one is active, it can inhibit the other. If the amygdala's response is strong and swift, it can override the prefrontal cortex, leading to impulsive, emotionally driven actions. Conversely, a well-functioning prefrontal cortex can temper the amygdala's reactions, allowing for more rational and thoughtful responses.

In emotionally charged situations, the amygdala might react first, triggering a strong emotional response. However, with a brief pause, the prefrontal cortex can catch up, evaluate the situation, and help us respond more balanced and effectively.

For instance, think back to the earlier example of the dark alley. Upon hearing the rustling sound, your amygdala's initial reaction might be fear, triggering a fight-or-flight response. However, your prefrontal cortex takes a moment to assess the situation rationally. It might realize that the rustling sound was simply a cat rummaging through a trash can, and there's no real threat. This rational assessment calms your initial fear, and you continue walking with a relieved sigh.

Understanding the amygdala and prefrontal cortex interplay is key to enhancing emotional intelligence. It empowers us to manage our emotional responses effectively, ensuring they serve us rather than sabotage us.

As we wrap up this chapter, remember the balance between the amygdala and the prefrontal cortex. Recognize the value of quick emotional responses and rational decision-making. Most importantly, remember that emotional intelligence is a skill we can develop and improve. Like a muscle, it strengthens with training and practice. So, let's continue exploring, learning, and growing together, harnessing emotional intelligence's power for a happier, healthier, and more fulfilling life.

NAVIGATING THE EMOTIONAL LANDSCAPE OF RELATIONSHIPS

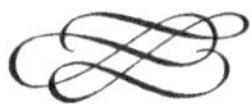

IMAGINE STANDING at the edge of a vast forest, the air around you humming with the sounds of life. Each rustle in the undergrowth, bird calls echoing in the trees, and wisps of wind rustling the leaves tell a story. But to understand these stories, you need to learn the language of the forest. The same goes for our emotions in relationships. Every glance, every tone of voice, and every gesture is like a signal in this emotional forest, telling us a story about our feelings and those of others. To navigate this landscape effectively, we need to learn the language of emotional signals.

DECODING EMOTIONAL SIGNALS IN RELATIONSHIPS

Recognizing Emotional Cues

Emotional cues are like signposts in our emotional landscape. They can come from within us, such as a knot in our stomach when we're anxious, or from others, like a friend's silence when they're upset. Recognizing these cues is the first step in decoding emotional signals.

It's like when you're watching a movie, and you notice the protagonist's clenched jaw or hear the tremble in her voice. You don't need her to say she's angry or scared; the cues speak for themselves. Similarly, in everyday interactions, we can pick up on subtle emotional cues that give us insight into our and others' emotional states.

Consider a scenario where your partner comes home from work, slumps on the couch, and sighs deeply. Even without them saying a word, you recognize the emotional cues (the slump and the sigh), signaling that they've had a tough day.

Understanding Non-Verbal Communication

Non-verbal communication is a powerful transmitter of emotional signals. It includes body language, facial expressions, tone of voice, and even the pace of speech. Research suggests that a significant portion of our communication is non-verbal, making it a critical aspect of emotional intelligence.

Have you ever walked into a room and immediately sensed the mood, even though no one said a word? That's non-verbal communication at work. It's the folded arms of a coworker during a meeting, the soft tone your friend uses when she's comforting you, or the quickened speech pace of your sibling when they're excited.

Let's say you're at a family gathering. Your aunt maintains a rigid posture and avoids eye contact when the topic of her job is mentioned. Despite her insistence that everything is "fine," her nonverbal communication tells a different story, indicating discomfort or unease.

Responding to Emotional Needs

Recognizing emotional cues and understanding nonverbal communication are crucial in decoding emotional signals. However, responding appropriately to these signals and addressing the emotional needs they signify are equally important.

Returning to the earlier example where your partner comes home from a tough day at work, an appropriate response might be to offer a comforting presence, ask if they want to talk about it, or give them some space, depending on their preferences.

Imagine your friend opens up about feeling overwhelmed by her workload. Recognizing her emotional cues and understanding her non-verbal communication, you acknowledge her feelings, "It sounds like you're under a lot of pressure," offering validation. You might then ask, "How can I support you?" addressing her emotional needs.

Decoding emotional signals in relationships is like learning a new language. It takes patience, practice, and time. But as we become more fluent, we can navigate our relationships with greater understanding, empathy, and connection. We understand the 'stories' each emotional signal tells, enabling us to respond appropriately and build stronger, more emotionally intelligent relationships.

Remember, emotional intelligence isn't about fixing or changing emotions - ours or anyone else's. It's about understanding, accepting, and responding to these emotions in a way that respects our emotional needs and those of others. By learning the language of emotional signals, we can bring more compassion, empathy, and understanding into our relationships, enriching our emotional landscape and strengthening our connections with others.

THE STRENGTH OF EMPATHY

Empathetic Listening

Let's start with a scenario. Imagine a relative or a close friend sharing a dilemma with you, her words laced with uncertainty and concern. You don't interrupt, offer advice, or judge as she speaks. You listen. This active engagement is what we call empathetic listening.

Empathetic listening is like a soothing balm for a worried soul. It gives the speaker a safe space to express their thoughts and feelings without fear of judgment or criticism. It's not about agreeing or disagreeing, fixing or advising; it's about being present, accepting, and understanding.

Think of empathetic listening as a two-step process. The first step is to listen with your ears—to hear the words. The second step is to listen with your heart—to understand the emotions behind those words. This process can create a profound connection between you and the speaker when done genuinely and gracefully.

Empathetic Responding

The second aspect of empathy is empathetic responding. This goes hand in hand with compassionate listening and involves responding to the speaker's emotions to show understanding and acceptance.

Empathetic responding isn't about providing solutions or giving advice. It's about acknowledging and validating the other person's feelings. It's saying, "I hear you. I understand you. Your feelings matter."

Let's go back to the scenario with your relative or friend. After she finishes sharing her dilemma, you don't immediately jump in with advice or share a similar experience. Instead, you might say something like, "That sounds tough. I can understand why you're feeling stressed." This empathetic response acknowledges her feelings and validates her experience, making her feel seen and understood.

Empathy in Conflict Resolution

Conflicts are a part of life. They can occur in relationships, professional interactions, and even within ourselves. When faced with conflict, our first instinct might be to defend our position, prove our point, or win the argument. But what if we tried a different approach? What if we used empathy to navigate conflicts?

When conflicts arise, emotions often run high. It's easy to get caught up in the heat of the moment, losing sight of the other person's feelings and perspectives. But this is where empathy can make a difference. By taking a step back and trying to understand the other person's emotions and viewpoints, we can respond to conflicts more effectively.

Suppose you and your partner disagree about how to handle a financial issue. Instead of digging in and insisting on your way, you pause and listen to your partner's concerns. You try to understand where they're coming from and why they feel like they do. Your empathetic approach diffuses the tension, opening up a more productive and respectful discussion space.

Empathy, in its essence, is about connection. It's about bridging the gap between our internal world and the world of others. By practicing empathetic listening, responding, and conflict resolution, we can deepen our connections, improve our relationships, and enhance our emotional intelligence.

Remember, empathy isn't a switch we can turn on and off at will. It's more like a muscle that we can strengthen with practice. Like any other muscle, it requires patience, persistence, and grace. So, let's keep practicing, learning, and growing. With each step we take, we're becoming more emotionally intelligent and building more robust, more fulfilling relationships. And isn't that a beautiful thing?

EMOTIONAL INTELLIGENCE AND CONFLICT RESOLUTION

Identifying Emotional Triggers in Conflicts

Just as a spark can ignite a fire, emotional triggers can ignite conflict. These triggers are personal and unique to each of us, linked to our past experiences, values, and vulnerabilities. Certain words, actions, or situations might elicit strong emotional reactions from us.

Let's imagine that you and your colleagues are in a group discussion at work, and you present an idea you've been working on for weeks. A colleague dismisses it with a flippant comment, and before you know it, you're in the throes of a heated argument. In this case, your colleague's dismissive attitude towards your hard work might trigger you emotionally.

Identifying our emotional triggers is like mapping our emotional terrain. It helps us anticipate and prepare for potential conflicts, enabling us to navigate them more effectively.

Using Emotionally Intelligent Communication

The way we communicate during a conflict can either fuel the fire or douse the flames. Emotionally intelligent communication involves expressing our feelings and needs clearly and respectfully, listening to understand rather than to reply, and seeking win-win solutions that respect everyone's needs and feelings.

There may have been a time when you and your partner disagreed about chores. Instead of blaming or criticizing, you express your feelings using "I" statements, such as "I feel overwhelmed when I have to do all the chores myself. I need us to share the responsibilities equally." This type of communication not only expresses your feelings and needs but does so in a non-confrontational way that invites cooperation rather than conflict.

Applying Emotional Intelligence to Resolve and Prevent Conflicts

Resolving conflicts requires us to apply all the elements of emotional intelligence—self-awareness, self-regulation, empathy, and effective communication. It's about understanding our feelings and those of others, managing our emotional responses, and communicating in a way that leads to resolution rather than escalation.

Let's go back to the workplace scenario. After the heated argument with your colleague, you take a moment to understand your feelings and identify your emotional triggers. You then approach your colleague, calmly expressing your feelings and explaining why her comment upset you. You also listen to her perspective and understand her feelings. Together, you find a solution that respects both your viewpoints.

Similarly, emotional intelligence can also help prevent conflicts. By improving our self-awareness, we can recognize and manage our emotional triggers before they ignite a conflict. Enhancing our empathy, we can understand others' feelings and perspectives, reducing misunderstandings. And by improving our communication skills, we can express our needs and emotions in a way that fosters cooperation rather than conflict.

The path of emotional intelligence isn't always easy. It requires us to explore our emotional depths, challenge our habitual responses, and step into others' shoes. But it's a path worth taking, leading to healthier, more fulfilling relationships and a more balanced, peaceful state of mind. And isn't that something worth striving for? So, let's keep moving forward, one step at a time, knowing that with each step, we're becoming more emotionally intelligent and building a life of deeper connection, understanding, and fulfillment.

BUILDING TRUST WITH EMOTIONAL INTELLIGENCE

Trust is the bedrock of any enduring relationship. It creates a safe space for vulnerability, open communication, and deeper connections. Trust takes time to grow like a tree, but it provides a sturdy base for the relationship to flourish once established. Emotional intelligence can be a powerful tool in nurturing this growth, mainly through emotional honesty, consistency, and understanding.

Emotional Honesty

Honesty is a cornerstone of trust. It extends beyond telling the truth to being open and genuine about our feelings. Emotional honesty is the willingness to acknowledge and share our emotions, even when uncomfortable or challenging. It's about removing our emotional masks and showing up as our authentic selves.

Imagine you're overwhelmed with work, but your friend asks for help on a project. Instead of saying yes and adding to your stress, emotional honesty would involve expressing your feelings: "I'd love to help, but I'm swamped with work right now and can't take on anything more." This honesty clarifies your boundaries and builds trust, as your friend knows she can rely on you to be truthful about your capacity and feelings.

Emotional Consistency

Another pillar of trust is consistency in our emotional responses. It involves managing our emotions predictably and reliably. Emotional consistency doesn't mean suppressing our feelings or pretending everything is fine when it's not. It means being aware of our emotions, managing them effectively, and responding to situations that align with our values and commitments.

Envision a situation in which you've had a challenging day at work, and your partner forgets to do something you asked them to. While letting your frustration spill over into your reaction can be tempting, emotional consistency involves managing your response and expressing your disappointment calmly and constructively. This consistency in your emotional reactions builds trust, as your partner can predict your responses and feel secure in your emotional stability.

Emotional Support and Understanding

Support and understanding are vital components of trust. When we show emotional support, we say, "I'm here for you, no matter what." When we offer emotional understanding, we say, "I see your feelings, and they matter." Both these messages help build a strong foundation of trust.

Let's say a close friend shares that she's going through a difficult breakup. Emotional support might look like offering a listening ear, sending encouraging messages, or simply being there for her. Emotional understanding, on the other hand, might involve acknowledging her feelings of sadness and heartbreak, validating her emotions, and refraining from rushing her healing process. This support and understanding can significantly strengthen the trust in your relationship as your friend knows she can rely on you during tough times.

Building trust is not an overnight process. It's a gradual, ongoing effort that requires patience, commitment, and emotional intelligence. By practicing emotional honesty, consistency, and understanding, we can nurture trust in our relationships, creating a safe and secure emotional environment for ourselves and others. It's a beautiful endeavor that leads to deeper connections, richer interactions, and a stronger sense of emotional well-being.

As we wrap up this chapter, let's take a moment to reflect. Emotional intelligence isn't a destination; it's a pathway we continually walk, learning and growing with each step we take. It's a pathway that leads to healthier relationships, better conflict resolution, and deeper trust. As we walk this path, we improve our relationships, emotional health, and well-being. So, let's keep walking, growing, and exploring the beautiful landscape of emotional intelligence. As we step into the next chapter, we'll look at how emotional intelligence can guide us in managing stress, a vital aspect of our mental health. So, let's take a deep breath and continue on our path.

BREAKING THE TIES BETWEEN STRESS AND EMOTIONAL INTELLIGENCE

CLOSE YOUR EYES. Picture a teapot bubbling away on a stove. As the heat intensifies, pressure builds within the teapot. It starts to make its whistling sound, a clear signal that it's time to reduce the heat. Now, imagine the teapot is you, and the heat is stress. Just as the whistle signals the teapot's threshold, your body and mind show signs when stress levels rise too high. It's time we learned to listen to those signals, to understand and manage the heat - our stress.

In this chapter, we'll explore the landscape of stress, identifying common triggers that crank up the heat in our lives. We'll also discuss how enhancing our emotional intelligence can help us manage stress effectively, just as lowering the heat prevents the teapot from boiling over.

IDENTIFYING STRESS TRIGGERS

Personal Relationships

Personal relationships can be a source of joy and fulfillment but can also increase stress levels. Conflicts with a partner, misunderstandings with a friend, or concerns over a child's behavior can all trigger stress. It's like being on a roller coaster ride, experiencing the highs of love and connection but also the lows of discord and worry.

Work Deadlines

Work deadlines are like ticking time bombs of stress. The incessant ticking is the constant reminder of tasks to be completed, projects to be handled, and deadlines to be met. Each tick amplifies the pressure, pushing your stress levels higher.

Financial Worries

Financial worries can cast long shadows over our peace of mind. They're like constant background noise, always there, constantly gnawing at you. Whether it's anxiety over paying bills, stress about saving for the future, or concern about job stability, financial worries can significantly contribute to stress.

Health Concerns

Health concerns, whether about our health or that of a loved one, can be potent stress triggers. They're like dark clouds on the horizon, looming with potential storms of worry, fear, and uncertainty.

Lack of Time

The feeling of not having enough time is an everyday stress trigger. It's like running a race against a clock, always trying to outrun the ticking hands. The constant rush, the never-ending to-do lists, and the struggle to balance various responsibilities can make us feel stressed and overwhelmed.

Identifying these stress triggers is like marking the spots where the heat flares up in our lives. Once we know where the hotspots are, we can use our emotional intelligence to manage them effectively. So, let's keep going, exploring how emotional intelligence can turn down the heat and help us navigate stress with greater ease and resilience.

THE ROLE OF EMOTIONAL INTELLIGENCE IN STRESS MANAGEMENT

Self-Awareness

Picture yourself on an ocean beach, sitting in the sand on the banks of a rolling ocean. You can hear the waves lapping at the shoreline with your eyes closed. Each rush of water in the ocean tells you something about the power of those waves. This intuition is similar to self-awareness in the topic of emotional intelligence. It's a deep understanding of our emotions and an innate ability to identify our feelings and why. It's the first point of contact with our emotional world, the initial step in managing stress.

Think of a time when you may have been preparing for a presentation at work. You notice a flutter in your stomach and a quickening of your heartbeat. That's self-awareness, recognizing the onset of stress. By identifying these initial signs, you're better positioned to manage the impending stress, maybe through deep breathing, a quick walk, or a few minutes of mindfulness.

Emotional Regulation

Imagine emotional regulation as the thermostat in a room, maintaining a comfortable and steady temperature despite changes in the weather outside. It's the skill of adjusting our responses to emotions to keep us balanced and aligned with our values. Just as a well-functioning thermostat prevents extremes such as freezing or overheating, effective emotional regulation helps us stay composed and navigate the highs and lows of stress with resilience.

Remembering the presentation scenario, let's say you keep cool despite your initial nervousness. You take a few deep breaths, visualize your success, and step onto the stage with confidence. That's emotional regulation, managing your stress response to perform under pressure.

Empathy

Empathy has two roles in stress management. First, it involves being empathetic toward ourselves and showing self-compassion and understanding. Second, it recognizes stress signals and responds with kindness and support. This dual role can alleviate stress, fostering a sense of connection and shared humanity.

Imagine a friend confiding in you about her stress over an upcoming project. You listen empathetically, validating her feelings of anxiety and offering reassurance. This empathetic interaction helps your friend feel supported and reinforces your ability to manage stress, building a sense of shared resilience.

Motivation

When we think of motivation, we often think of achieving our goals or overcoming challenges. However, motivation also plays a crucial role in stress management and emotional intelligence. The drive propels us to act against stress and seek strategies and tools to help us manage stress effectively.

Let's say you notice that your stress levels have been high lately. Motivated to improve your well-being, you start exploring stress management strategies. You try out yoga, start a journal, or perhaps seek guidance from a counselor. Your motivation, a testament to your emotional intelligence, fuels this proactive approach to managing stress.

Social Skills

Last, let's discuss social skills, an often overlooked aspect of stress management. Social skills refer to our ability to communicate our feelings, seek support, and offer help to others. These skills can foster a support network, a sense of belonging, and shared resilience against stress.

Picture yourself feeling stressed about a personal issue. You reach out to a trusted friend, expressing your feelings and concerns. Your friend listens, offers comfort, and shares her own experiences. This exchange helps you feel less alone and strengthens your bond, building a supportive relationship to buffer against future stress.

To review, emotional intelligence isn't just about understanding and managing emotions. It's about using this understanding to navigate life's challenges, especially stress, with greater resilience and skill. It's about tapping into our self-awareness, emotional regulation, empathy, motivation, and social skills to manage stress effectively. As we enhance our emotional intelligence, we become better equipped to handle stress, improve our overall well-being, build stronger relationships, and live a more fulfilled and balanced life. So, let's keep learning, growing, and exploring the beautiful landscape of emotional intelligence. The journey continues, and it is well worth the effort.

STRESS REACTION TO STRESS MANAGEMENT TECHNIQUES

Deep Breathing Exercises

When stressed, our breath can become erratic, like a kite buffeted by strong winds. Deep breathing exercises are the string that tethers the kite, helping us regain control, stabilize our nervous system, and find calm. It's like gently pulling the kite back to steady it in the sky, bringing us back to the present and allowing us to relax.

One simple deep breathing exercise is the '4-7-8' technique. Here's how to do the exercise:

- Close your eyes and take a moment to observe your natural breath.
- Slowly inhale through your nose for a count of four.
- Hold your breath for a count of seven.
- Exhale through your mouth for a count of eight.
- Repeat this cycle four times.

This technique calms your mind and shifts your focus from the source of stress to your breath, providing immediate relief.

Progressive Muscle Relaxation

Stress often leaves our muscles tense and tight. Progressive muscle relaxation (PMR) releases this tension, promoting physical relaxation and mental calm. It's like giving yourself a gentle massage, easing the knots of stress in your body.

PMR involves tensing and then relaxing different muscle groups in your body. Start with your toes and move up to your legs, stomach, hands, arms, shoulders, neck, and face. As you tense each muscle group, hold for a count of five and then release. As you progress, you might notice a sense of deep relaxation spreading through your body, a sign that the technique is working.

Visualization Techniques

Visualization is a powerful stress management tool. It's about creating a mental sanctuary where stress cannot reach. Whether it's a serene beach, a lush forest, or a cozy room, this mental haven can provide a much-needed respite from stress.

Find a quiet place, close your eyes, and imagine your sanctuary. Engage all your senses - this place's sights, sounds, smells, and feelings. The more vivid your visualization, the more relaxing it will be. With practice, you'll find that simply visiting this mental sanctuary can help lower your stress levels.

Cognitive Reframing

Cognitive reframing is a mental gymnastics routine. It involves flipping our perspective, turning stress-inducing thoughts into stress-relieving ones. It does not include denying reality but viewing it through a more balanced, positive lens.

For instance, if you're stressed about an upcoming presentation, you might think, "I'm going to mess up," or "What if they don't like my ideas?" Cognitive reframing involves changing these thoughts to "I'm prepared, and I'll do my best" or "I believe in my ideas, and I'll present them confidently." This shift in perspective can significantly reduce stress, empowering you to face challenges with a positive mindset.

Assertive Communication

Assertive communication is a crucial skill in stress management. It's about expressing our feelings and needs clearly and respectfully, without aggression or passivity. It's like building a bridge of understanding, connecting our emotional world with that of others.

For example, you could use assertive communication instead of silence or complaining about your workload if you feel stressed due to an overloaded work schedule. You might approach your supervisor and say, "I value my work and want to perform at my best. However, the current workload is causing a lot of stress. Could we look at how to balance it better?" Open, respectful communication can alleviate stress and improve relationships and overall well-being.

Remember, stress management isn't about eliminating stress. That would be like trying to calm the ocean—an impossible task. Instead, it's about learning to surf the waves of stress using tools like deep breathing, progressive muscle relaxation, visualization, cognitive reframing, and assertive communication. So, let's keep practicing these techniques, turn the heat down on our stress levels, and nurture our emotional health and well-being.

Visualization Techniques

Imagine yourself stepping into a beautiful, tranquil garden. The sun is gently warming your skin, a soft breeze rustles the leaves, and the air is filled with the soothing sound of a babbling brook. This serene image is a lovely daydream and a powerful visualization technique. Visualization creates a peaceful sanctuary in your mind, a place to retreat when stress levels rise. It's like having a personal oasis of calm, accessible anytime.

To practice visualization, find a quiet space and close your eyes. Take a few deep breaths to center yourself, then create your tranquil image. It could be a garden, a beach, a forest, or any place that brings you peace. Engage all your senses in this visualization - your peaceful place's sights, sounds, smells, and sensations. As you immerse yourself in this sanctuary, you'll likely notice your stress melting away, replaced by a deep sense of calm.

Cognitive Reframing

Picture a pair of glasses with tinted lenses. These lenses change how you see the world, adding a tint of color to everything you see. Imagine these glasses represent your thoughts; the tint is your perspective. Cognitive reframing is like changing the tint on your glasses, altering your perspective to manage stress better.

It's about challenging and changing stress-inducing thoughts. For example, if you're stressed about making a mistake, you might think, "If I mess up, it'll be a disaster." Cognitive reframing changes this thought to "Even if I make a mistake, I'll learn from it and improve." This shift in perspective can significantly reduce stress, helping you view challenges as opportunities for growth.

Assertive Communication

Assertive communication is like a bridge, connecting your feelings and needs with those of others. It's about expressing yourself clearly and respectfully without being aggressive or passive. When faced with stress, especially in interpersonal situations, assertive communication can be a powerful tool.

For instance, if you're feeling stressed because a colleague constantly delegates their tasks to you, you could use assertive communication instead of silently bearing the extra workload or lashing out in frustration. You might say, "I've noticed that I've been taking on many of your tasks lately. I'm happy to help when possible, but this is starting to impact my work." This respectful, straightforward communication can help resolve the situation, reduce stress, and foster better relationships.

These techniques reduce stress, enhance emotional intelligence, build resilience, and empower us to lead happier, healthier lives. This transformative process enriches not only our own lives but also the lives of those around us.

MANAGING STRESS IN THE WORKPLACE

Dealing with Difficult Colleagues

Picture a bustling office. Amid the buzz of conversations and clatter of keyboards, there's a source of stress that's all too familiar—a challenging coworker. Perhaps the colleague never meets deadlines, communicates poorly, or doesn't contribute to team projects. This adds an extra layer of stress to the already demanding workplace environment.

So, how do we deal with this? The key is to develop a strategy rooted in empathy and assertiveness. Try to understand their perspective, even if it's hard. Maybe they're struggling with their workload or personal issues. An empathetic conversation could open doors for better understanding and collaboration. However, it's also essential to be assertive. If their behavior affects your work, communicate your concerns respectfully and honestly. It's not about confrontation; it's about setting boundaries and finding solutions.

Meeting Tight Deadlines

The ticking clock and the looming deadline—these scenarios can skyrocket stress levels. Effective time management and a balanced perspective are the key to managing this stress.

Start by breaking down large tasks into smaller, manageable parts and creating a realistic schedule. This approach makes the workload feel less overwhelming and provides a clear roadmap to meeting the deadline.

Also, remember that while deadlines are important, they're not worth compromising your mental health. If a deadline is unrealistic, discuss it with your supervisor. Often, accommodations can be made.

Balancing Work and Personal Life

Picture a tightrope walker. Their professional life, which is filled with responsibilities and deadlines, is on one side, while their personal lives, family, hobbies, and relaxation time are on the other. The challenge is maintaining balance, ensuring one side doesn't overshadow the other.

Achieving this balance involves setting clear boundaries, such as specific work hours and dedicated personal time. It also means taking care of your health, ensuring you're physically and mentally equipped to handle both sides of your life. Remember, it's not about choosing work over personal life or vice versa but finding a sustainable balance that caters to both.

Handling Job Insecurity

Job insecurity can be a significant source of stress, casting a shadow of uncertainty over our professional lives. The fear of losing our jobs, whether due to organizational changes, economic conditions, or personal performance, can be overwhelming.

Dealing with this fear involves focusing on what you can control. Continue demonstrating your work value, improving your skills, and maintaining a positive attitude. At the same time, having a backup plan can provide a sense of security. This could involve saving for a rainy day, updating your resume, or networking within your industry.

Coping with Organizational Changes

Organizational changes, such as management shifts, restructuring, or new policies, can trigger stress. It's like suddenly finding yourself in unfamiliar territory, unsure of what lies ahead.

Navigating this terrain involves staying flexible and open to changes, maintaining clear communication with your supervisors, and focusing on the constants amidst the changes. Remember, change is a part of life, and your ability to adapt is a testament to your resilience and emotional intelligence.

In the end, workplace stress is inevitable. However, with emotional intelligence, we can learn to manage this stress, turning challenges into opportunities for growth. Rather than letting stress control us, we can take charge, using our self-awareness, emotional regulation, empathy, motivation, and social skills to navigate the workplace with resilience and grace.

So, let's bid goodbye to the "boiling teapot" scenario. With the right skills and mindset, you can handle the heat, turning the flame down when it rises too high. You've got this, and remember, you're not alone in this. We're in this together, learning, growing, and becoming more emotionally intelligent daily. In the next chapter, we'll explore how emotional intelligence can help us overcome negative self-talk in another critical aspect of our lives.

OVERCOMING NEGATIVE SELF-TALK

CLOSE YOUR EYES and imagine you're standing before a mirror. As you gaze at your reflection, a voice whispers, "You're not good enough. You can't do it." This voice, as familiar as it is unkind, is your negative self-talk. It's a critical inner voice that can cloud our thoughts, dampen our spirits, and hinder our progress. This chapter will explore how emotional intelligence can help us challenge and change this narrative, replacing negative self-talk with positive affirmations.

THE POWER OF SELF-TALK

Self-talk, our ongoing internal dialogue with ourselves, can profoundly influence various aspects of our lives, from self-confidence and decision-making to stress management and relationship-building.

Self-Confidence

Think of self-confidence as a plant. Positive self-talk is the water that nurtures this plant, helping it grow and flourish. When we tell ourselves, "I can handle this," or "I have the skills to succeed," we're watering our plant of self-confidence, strengthening it from the roots up.

Decision-Making

Self-talk can also guide our decision-making process. Positive self-talk can provide reassurance and clarity when faced with a difficult decision. It's like having a supportive friend in our corner whispering, "Trust your instincts," or "You've made tough choices before; you can do this."

Problem-Solving

Problem-solving often involves overcoming obstacles and thinking creatively. Positive self-talk can fuel this process as a motivational coach encourages us to keep going. The voice says, "This is tough, but I can figure it out," or "Every problem has a solution."

Stress Management

When stressed, our self-talk can amplify or help alleviate the pressure. Positive self-talk can create a soothing mantra that helps us navigate stressful situations. The calming voice reminds us, "This is temporary," or "I can handle this."

Relationship Building

Our self-talk can influence how we interact with others. Positive self-talk makes us more likely to approach our relationships with kindness, patience, and understanding. It's like an internal pep talk that encourages us to "Treat others with respect" or "Listen before you respond."

Positive self-talk can be a powerful tool for boosting self-confidence and enhancing relationships. However, it can be challenging to silence negative self-talk and amplify the positive. This is where emotional intelligence comes into play, offering strategies for managing self-talk effectively.

EMOTIONAL INTELLIGENCE: THE KEY TO TAMING NEGATIVE SELF-TALK

Self-Awareness

Imagine your mind as a garden. In this garden, each thought is a seed. Some seeds grow into beautiful flowers, while others grow into thorny weeds. Self-awareness is the gardener's knowledge and understanding of which seeds to water and which to weed out. It's about recognizing our negative self-talk, understanding its roots, and observing its impact on our emotions and actions.

Let's say you're preparing for a job interview, and a voice in your head whispers, "You're not qualified enough. They'll never hire you." That's negative self-talk. With self-awareness, you can identify this thought as it arises, understand that it stems from fear and self-doubt, and observe how it triggers feelings of anxiety and defeat. This recognition is the first step in managing negative self-talk.

Self-Regulation

Returning to our garden analogy, self-regulation involves weeding out the thorny plants and nurturing the beautiful flowers. It consists of managing negative self-talk, replacing it with positive affirmations, and controlling our emotional responses.

In the job interview scenario, self-regulation involves challenging the negative thought, "You're not qualified enough. They'll never hire you," and replacing it with a positive affirmation, "I am capable and well-prepared. I have a strong chance of getting this job." It's also about managing emotions, calming anxiety, and fostering confidence and optimism.

Motivation

In our garden of the mind, motivation is the sunshine that promotes growth. The driving force propels us to manage negative self-talk, overcome challenges, and strive for positive growth.

When faced with negative self-talk, your motivation might whisper, "This is tough, but I can handle it. I've overcome challenges before, and I can do it again." This motivational boost can give you the strength to manage negative self-talk, transforming it into a source of growth and resilience.

Empathy

Empathy, in the context of self-talk, is about being kind and understanding towards ourselves. It's about treating ourselves with the same compassion and understanding we would offer a friend.

When you catch yourself engaging in negative self-talk, empathy means saying to yourself, "It's okay. Everyone has self-doubts sometimes. It doesn't define my worth or ability." This self-empathy can soften the blow of negative self-talk, fostering self-acceptance and self-love.

Social Skills

Lastly, social skills are crucial in managing negative self-talk. This might seem surprising, as self-talk is a personal, internal process. However, social skills can influence how we talk to ourselves.

Consider a scenario where you make a mistake at work. Your negative self-talk might start criticizing you, "How could you mess up like this? You're so careless." However, consider how you would respond if a colleague made the same mistake. You'd likely be understanding and supportive, saying, "Mistakes happen. You'll do better next time." Applying these social skills to our self-talk, treating ourselves with the same kindness and understanding we offer others, can help manage negative self-talk.

As you've read, we can effectively manage our negative self-talk by leveraging our self-awareness, self-regulation, motivation, empathy, and social skills. By cultivating these aspects of emotional intelligence, we can transform the "thorny garden" of negative self-talk into a "blooming garden" of positivity, resilience, and self-compassion. This is a beautiful transformation, one that enhances not just our mental well-being but also our overall quality of life.

PRACTICAL TECHNIQUES FOR POSITIVE SELF-TALK

Affirmations

Think of affirmations as tiny seeds of positivity that you plant in the garden of your mind. When nurtured with belief and repetition, each seed can grow into a robust tree of positive self-talk. Affirmations are positive statements that can help you challenge and overcome negative thoughts. They are like the sunlight that nourishes the seeds, guiding their growth toward positivity and resilience.

An effective affirmation is upbeat, personal, and specific in the present tense. For example, instead of saying, "I will be confident," say, "I am confident." Repeat your affirmations daily, preferably aloud and in front of a mirror. The more you hear and see yourself voicing these affirmations, the stronger they root in your subconscious, gradually transforming your negative self-talk into a positive narrative.

Gratitude Journaling

Picture yourself holding a magnifying glass, highlighting all the good things in your life. Gratitude journaling does this. It shifts your focus from negative thoughts to positive experiences, cultivating an attitude of appreciation and positivity.

Start by setting aside a few minutes daily to write in your gratitude journal. Note down three things you are grateful for each day, no matter how small they might seem. It could be a warm cup of coffee, a kind gesture from a stranger, or a challenging experience that led to personal growth. As you fill the pages of your journal, your negative self-talk will soften, replaced by a narrative of gratitude and positivity.

Mindfulness

Mindfulness is like a gentle anchor that holds you steady in the present moment. It's a state of active, open attention to the present, where you observe your thoughts and feelings from a distance without judging them as good or bad.

Mindfulness can help you become more aware of your positive and negative self-talk. You can start with a simple mindfulness exercise: take a quiet moment, close your eyes, and focus on your breath. As thoughts and feelings arise, observe them without judgment or engagement. Over time, mindfulness can help you discern your self-talk patterns, providing valuable insights into managing negative thoughts and fostering positivity.

Cognitive Reframing

Imagine standing before a mirror that reflects your current and potential future self. Cognitive reframing is a technique for transforming negative or unhelpful thoughts into positive, constructive ones.

Cognitive reframing starts with identifying negative thoughts. For instance, "I can't do this" or "I'm not good enough." Once you've identified such a thought, challenge it. Ask yourself, "Is this thought accurate?" "Is there another way to view this situation?" "What advice would I give a friend in a similar situation?". By asking these questions, you can often find a more positive, realistic way to frame the situation, like "This is tough, but I can handle it," or "I'm learning and improving each day."

Self-Compassion

Self-compassion is about treating yourself with the kindness, understanding, and patience you would offer a friend. It's about acknowledging that everyone makes mistakes and experiences difficulties, and it's okay not to be perfect.

Next time you struggle or feel inadequate, try soothing yourself with comfort and encouragement instead of engaging in negative self-talk or criticism. Speak to yourself as you would to a friend in a similar situation. This shift from self-criticism to self-compassion can profoundly impact your self-talk, replacing negativity with understanding, kindness, and acceptance.

These practical techniques are tools in your emotional intelligence toolbox. They can help you cultivate positive self-talk, manage negative thoughts, and foster a healthier, more positive mindset. Just like any other skill, they require practice and patience. But as you continue to apply them, you'll notice a shift in your self-talk, outlook, and overall emotional well-being. So plant the seeds of positivity in your mind, water them with affirmations, gratitude, mindfulness, cognitive reframing, and self-compassion, and watch your garden of cheerful self-talk bloom.

TRANSITION FROM NEGATIVE TO POSITIVE SELF-TALK

Overcoming Impostor Syndrome

Impostor syndrome lurks in our minds, casting doubt on our abilities and achievements. It's the sneaky voice that whispers, "You're a fraud. You don't deserve your success." But here's the thing: that voice is wrong.

Let's take Sara, a bright, ambitious young woman who recently landed a high-profile job. Despite her qualifications and achievements, she often felt like an impostor, fearing that her colleagues would discover she was a 'fraud.' This negative self-talk was draining her confidence and joy.

Recognizing this pattern, Sara decided it was time for a change. She started by acknowledging her negative self-talk and understanding its roots. She realized that her impostor syndrome stemmed from a fear of failure and a deep-seated need to be perfect.

Next, Sara began challenging her negative self-talk. Whenever she thought, "I'm not good enough," she would counter it with, "I am competent and deserving of my position." Over time, these positive affirmations started drowning out the voice of impostor syndrome, bolstering Sara's confidence and self-esteem.

Dealing with Rejection

Rejection can sting, whether it's a job application, a romantic interest, or a social situation. It's like a punch in the gut that leaves us winded and questioning our worth. But remember, rejection is not a measure of your worth; it's merely a part of life.

Let's look at Jake, an aspiring writer who faced rejection after rejection from publishers. Each "no" felt like a personal attack, fueling his negative self-talk and making him question his talent.

However, Jake decided to reframe his perspective. He recognized that rejection was an inevitable part of the writing process, not a reflection of his talent. He began to view each rejection as a stepping stone, not a roadblock. Instead of thinking, "I'm a failure," he would tell himself, "Every rejection brings me one step closer to acceptance."

Coping with Failure

Failure, like a bitter pill, can be hard to swallow. It can evoke feelings of disappointment, frustration, and self-doubt. But it's important to remember that failure is not the opposite of success; it's part of the journey to success.

Take Lily, for example, an entrepreneur whose first business venture failed. The experience left her feeling defeated, and her self-talk was filled with thoughts like, "I can't do anything right" or "I'm not cut out for this."

However, Lily chose to view her failure as a learning opportunity. She reflected on the missteps, gleaned valuable insights, and used them to fuel her next venture. Instead of criticizing herself for failing, she acknowledged her courage for trying, telling herself, "I'm proud of myself for taking risks. I'm learning and growing."

Building Self-Esteem

Self-esteem is about recognizing and appreciating our worth. It's like the foundation of a house: It supports and strengthens our sense of self. Negative self-talk can chip away at this foundation, but positive self-talk can help rebuild it.

Meet Mia, a teenager who struggles with low self-esteem. Mia regularly has negative thoughts like, "I'm not pretty enough" or "I'm not smart enough," dominating her self-talk. However, she decided to shift this narrative.

Mia started practicing self-compassion, treating herself with the same kindness and understanding she would offer a friend. She began challenging her negative self-talk, replacing it with positive affirmations like, "I am beautiful just as I am" and "I am intelligent and capable." Over time, these affirmations helped rebuild her self-esteem and transform her self-perception.

Enhancing Personal Relationships

Our self-talk can influence our relationships. Negative self-talk can create self-doubt, hinder communication, and strain relationships. On the other hand, positive self-talk can boost our confidence, improve our communication, and enhance our relationships.

Here's Sam, who often felt insecure in her relationship. Thoughts like, "He'll leave me" or "I'm not good enough for him" were frequent visitors in her self-talk. Recognizing the damage this was causing, Sam decided to make a change.

She began practicing mindfulness, observing her negative thoughts without judgment, and letting them pass. Sam also started using positive affirmations, telling herself, "I am loveable and deserving of love," and "I bring value to my relationship." This shift in self-talk enhanced Sam's confidence, improved her connection with her partner, and brought more joy to their relationship.

Ultimately, the transition from negative to positive self-talk is not a switch you flip overnight. It's a gradual process that requires patience, practice, and persistence. But it's a journey worth embarking on, as it can transform your self-perception, boost your confidence, and enhance your overall well-being.

So, let's remember Sara, Jake, Lily, Mia, and Sam—their struggles, triumphs, and journeys. Let's learn from them and apply these lessons in our lives. Let's continue to nurture our emotional intelligence, transform our self-talk, and foster our growth. As we move into the next chapter, remember you are capable, deserving, and enough. Let that be your mantra as we dive deeper into emotional intelligence.

CULTIVATING MINDFULNESS

IF YOU'VE EVER WATCHED a perennial garden grow, you know it's a slow, beautiful process that unfolds over time. Each day, the sun shines, the rain falls, and the plants reach a little higher, their roots burrowing deeper. This growth doesn't happen overnight; it requires time, patience, and the right conditions. The same goes for developing emotional intelligence. One of the most nurturing conditions for this growth is mindfulness.

Picture mindfulness as the sunlight that warms our emotional garden, helping us grow awareness, understanding, and control over our emotions. When mindful, we're fully present in the moment, aware of our thoughts, feelings, and sensations without judgment or distraction. This awareness is the fertile soil from which emotional intelligence grows, creating a vibrant landscape of self-understanding, empathy, and emotional regulation.

THE ROLE OF MINDFULNESS IN EMOTIONAL INTELLIGENCE

Stress Reduction

Imagine sitting by a calm lake, watching the gentle ripples on the surface. This serene scene mirrors the effect of mindfulness on stress. When mindful, we allow our thoughts and feelings to flow freely, like water in a lake. We observe them without getting swept up in them, reducing the intensity and impact of stress.

Think of a stressful day at work. You're juggling multiple tasks, answering endless emails, and dealing with unexpected challenges. Amid this whirlwind, you take a moment to practice mindfulness. You pause, take a deep breath, and observe your thoughts and feelings without judgment. This simple act can reduce the whirlwind of stress to a gentle breeze, helping you navigate your day with greater calm and clarity.

Enhanced Focus

Mindfulness is like a compass that points us toward the present moment. It helps us tune out distractions, enhancing our focus and attention. When mindful, we're fully engaged in what we're doing, whether listening to a friend, working on a task, or simply savoring a meal.

Think of times when you tried to concentrate on a task, but your mind was elsewhere. Perhaps you were worrying about an upcoming meeting, replaying a conversation, or planning your weekend. This mental chatter can scatter our focus, making concentrating on the task difficult. However, practicing mindfulness can quiet this chatter and sharpen our focus, like tuning a radio to eliminate static and hear the music.

Improved Emotional Regulation

Like the kite and its string, which we visited earlier in the book, mindfulness and emotional regulation go hand in hand. The kite represents our emotions, soaring high, dipping low, and fluttering in the wind. The string represents mindfulness, keeping the kite steady and preventing it from getting swept away by the gusts of emotional turbulence.

Let's say you're in a heated argument with a friend. Your emotions are rising, and you're on the verge of saying something you might regret. At that moment, you decide to practice mindfulness. You take a deep breath, observe your emotions, and recognize the urge to lash out as a passing storm, not a directive. This mindful moment can help you regulate your emotional response, choosing a more constructive way to express your feelings.

Increased Self-Compassion

Mindfulness fosters self-compassion, the ability to treat ourselves with kindness and understanding during difficult times. It's like a comforting blanket we wrap around ourselves through emotional storms.

Imagine you've made a mistake at work, and you're beating yourself up about it. Your mind is a swirl of self-critical thoughts like, "I'm such a failure," or "I can't do anything right." Practicing mindfulness can help you navigate this storm with self-compassion. You can acknowledge your disappointment without getting lost in self-criticism, reminding yourself that everyone makes mistakes and it is okay to be imperfect. This self-compassionate approach can soothe your emotional distress, helping you learn from the experience and move forward with kindness and understanding.

To reiterate, mindfulness is a powerful ally in our emotional intelligence journey. By cultivating mindfulness, we can reduce stress, enhance focus, improve emotional regulation, and foster self-compassion. Just like the sun nurtures the growth of a garden, mindfulness nurtures our emotional intelligence, helping us grow into more mindful, emotionally intelligent individuals. As we continue to practice and cultivate mindfulness, we'll find ourselves better equipped to navigate our emotions' beautiful, complex landscape.

PRACTICAL MINDFULNESS TECHNIQUES FOR EVERYDAY LIFE

Breath Awareness Meditation

Close your eyes and focus inward, noticing the natural rhythm of your breath. Feel the cool air entering your nostrils, filling your lungs, and the warm air leaving your body as you exhale. This is the essence of breath awareness meditation, a simple yet powerful mindfulness practice.

As you focus on your breath, you'll likely notice your mind quiet, your body relax, and your stress slowly melts. If your mind wanders, as it inevitably will, gently bring it back to your breath without judgment. Just as you would softly redirect a toddler who has strayed, guide your attention back to the sensation of breathing. This consistent practice can cultivate a deep sense of calm and present-moment awareness, strengthening your emotional intelligence.

Body Scan Technique

Imagine a gentle wave of awareness sweeping over your body, from the tips of your toes to the top of your head. The body scan technique is a mindfulness practice that invites you to tune into your body's sensations.

Lying comfortably, bring your attention to your toes. Notice any sensations you may feel—warmth, coolness, tension, or relaxation. Slowly move this awareness up through your feet, legs, torso, arms, and head. As you do this, you may encounter areas of tension or discomfort. Instead of avoiding these sensations, observe them with curiosity and acceptance. This mindful attention can help you reconnect with your body, fostering a harmonious mind-body relationship and enhancing emotional intelligence.

Mindful Eating Practice

Now, consider the act of eating, something we often do on autopilot. Mindful eating transforms this mundane act into a conscious experience, where we savor each bite with full attention and appreciation.

At your next meal, slow down and take a moment to appreciate the food before you. Notice the colors, the aroma, and the texture. As you take a bite, savor the taste, the crunch, the flavors. Chew slowly, noticing how the food changes as you chew. This mindful attention can enhance your enjoyment of the food, promote healthier eating habits, and be a delightful mindfulness practice.

Mindful Walking Exercise

Try turning it into a mindfulness exercise next time you walk, whether toward your office, neighborhood, or park. Instead of getting lost in thought or distracted by your surroundings, focus on the act of walking.

Feel the ground beneath your feet, your arms swing, and the rhythm of your steps. Notice the sensation of the air against your skin, the sounds around you, and the sights passing by. This practice, known as mindful walking, can transform a simple walk into a powerful mindfulness exercise, fostering present-moment awareness and tranquility.

Observing Thoughts Technique

Lastly, let's explore the observing thoughts technique, a mindfulness practice that encourages us to view our thoughts as passing clouds in the sky of our mind.

Sitting comfortably, close your eyes, and pay attention to your thoughts. Instead of engaging with them, observe them. Notice how they come and go and change; one thought leads to another. If you get caught up in an idea, gently bring your attention back to observing it.

This practice can provide valuable insights into your thought patterns, helping you better understand your mind. It also cultivates a sense of detachment from your thoughts, helping you realize that you are not your thoughts and don't have to react to every thought that arises.

These practical mindfulness techniques can significantly enhance your emotional intelligence when incorporated into your daily routine. By practicing breath awareness meditation, body scans, mindful eating, mindful walking, and observing thoughts, you cultivate mindfulness and foster self-awareness, improve focus, manage stress effectively, and nurture a compassionate relationship with yourself. So, go ahead, give these practices a try, and experience the profound impact of mindfulness on your emotional intelligence and overall well-being.

DEVELOPING SELF-AWARENESS THROUGH EMOTIONAL INTELLIGENCE

Journaling for Emotional Clarity

We've touched on journaling already in chapter four, and simply by putting pen to paper, your thoughts and feelings will flow freely, unfiltered, and unedited. This simple act of writing in a journal can be a powerful tool in building self-awareness. It's a private dialogue with yourself and an opportunity to explore your emotions in a safe space. I can't stress enough how empowering it is to collect your thoughts in a journal and revisit those journal entries sometime later. The journal entries are reminders of who we once were and stark reminders that refining our ability to practice emotional intelligence produces fantastic results.

Think about times when you felt emotionally overwhelmed, and your thoughts seemed tangled and chaotic. Writing in a journal can help unscramble these thoughts, providing clarity and insight. It's like untangling a knotted string—as you write about your feelings, the knots loosen, revealing the underlying emotions and thoughts.

The beauty of journaling lies in its flexibility. You can write about your day, express your hopes and dreams, vent your frustrations, or let your thoughts wander. The aim is to deepen your connection with your emotional self, enhancing your understanding and acceptance of your feelings.

Emotional Trigger Identification

We all have emotional triggers, specific situations, or behaviors that elicit strong emotional reactions. Identifying these triggers is a critical step in developing self-awareness.

Think of your emotional triggers as buttons. When someone or something presses these buttons, your emotions flare up. It could be a dismissive comment that sparks anger, a rejection that triggers hurt, or a stressful situation that induces anxiety.

Recognizing these triggers is like mapping your emotional terrain. It helps you anticipate emotional reactions and prepare effective responses. The goal isn't to eliminate these triggers but to manage them to align with your emotional intelligence and well-being.

Reflection on Emotional Responses

Reflection is a mirror that reflects your emotional responses, allowing you to understand and learn from them. It involves looking back at your emotional reactions, analyzing what caused them, how you expressed them, and their consequences.

Consider a time when you reacted strongly to a situation. In hindsight, you might realize that stress, tiredness, or past experiences influenced your reaction. Reflecting on this can help you understand why you reacted the way you did and how you might respond differently.

Reflection is not about self-judgment or regret. It's about self-understanding and growth. It's about learning from our past to enhance our future, fostering emotional intelligence.

Regular Check-ins with Self

In our busy lives, losing touch with our emotional selves is easy. Regular self-check-ins can help maintain this connection. It's like touching base with a friend, asking, "How am I feeling right now? What do I need?"

These check-ins don't need to be lengthy or complicated. They could be a quiet moment in the morning when you tune into your feelings, a pause in the afternoon to breathe and center yourself, or a few reflective minutes in the evening when you review your day.

The aim is to stay connected with your emotional self, recognizing and honoring your feelings as they arise. This ongoing dialogue with yourself fosters self-awareness, a cornerstone of emotional intelligence.

To review, cultivating self-awareness through emotional intelligence involves journaling for emotional clarity, identifying emotional triggers, reflecting on emotional responses, and conducting regular self-check-ins. Incorporating these practices into our daily lives can significantly enhance our emotional intelligence. They help us understand and navigate our emotional landscape with better skill and confidence, fostering emotional health and well-being.

MINDFULNESS IN ACTION

Stress Management

Meet Laura. Laura loves her job as a high school teacher, but it also comes with stress. Balancing lesson planning, grading assignments, and managing a lively bunch of teenagers can feel like a juggling act, leaving her feeling stressed and overwhelmed.

Laura discovered mindfulness as a way to manage her stress. She started with short, five-minute mindfulness exercises in the mornings, focusing on her breath and grounding herself for the day. This simple practice helped her begin her day calmly and positively.

When noise levels rose or unexpected challenges arose in the classroom, she would take a few mindful breaths, allowing her to respond calmly and composed. This mindfulness practice became her anchor, helping her navigate the turbulent seas of stress with greater ease and resilience.

Enhancing Focus

Now, let's consider the case of Raj, a software engineer. Raj's work involves complex problem-solving and requires intense focus. However, he is easily distracted and lets his mind wander during critical tasks.

Raj decided to try mindfulness to improve his focus. He incorporated mindful moments into his workday, taking short breaks to practice breath awareness or do a quick body scan. These practices helped him tune out distractions and return his attention to the task.

Over time, Raj noticed a significant improvement in his focus and productivity. Mindfulness enhanced his ability to concentrate and made him more aware of when his mind started wandering, enabling him to guide it back gently.

Emotional Regulation

Finally, let's look at Lisa, a customer service representative. Lisa's job involves dealing with disgruntled customers, which can be emotionally draining. She often reacts impulsively to rude customers, later regretting her responses.

Lisa turned to mindfulness as a tool to improve her emotional regulation. She started practicing mindfulness meditation daily, which gave her a sense of calm and balance.

When dealing with demanding customers, Lisa used her mindfulness skills to stay grounded at work. She learned to pause, take a mindful breath, and respond rather than react. This cautious approach transformed her customer interactions, allowing her to handle difficult situations gracefully and professionally.

These case studies highlight the power of mindfulness in real-life scenarios. Mindfulness can be transformative, whether managing stress, enhancing focus, or improving emotional regulation. As seen in the lives of Laura, Raj, and Lisa, mindfulness is more than just a concept; it's a practical skill that can significantly improve our emotional intelligence and overall quality of life.

As we wrap up this chapter, let's pause and take a mindful breath. Feel the air entering your nostrils, filling your lungs, and leaving your body. It's a simple act that brings you back to the present moment, the essence of mindfulness. Let's carry this essence with us as we move forward, infusing our lives with mindfulness and fostering emotional intelligence. The next chapter will explore how emotional intelligence can enhance our relationships, further enriching our lives.

THE HEARTBEAT OF OUR RELATIONSHIPS

When dealing with people, remember you are not dealing with creatures of logic but with creatures of emotion.

— DALE CARNEGIE

IMAGINE you're watching a beautifully choreographed ballet. The dancers move in harmony, their steps flawlessly synching with the rhythm of the music. This seamless synchronization mirrors emotional intelligence's role in our relationships. It's the rhythm that guides our interactions, the harmony that fosters understanding, and the grace that nurtures connection. To fully understand this rhythm, harmony, and grace, this chapter will tell us how emotional intelligence can transform our relationships.

EMOTIONAL INTELLIGENCE IN PERSONAL RELATIONSHIPS

Empathy in Family Dynamics

Consider a typical day in a family home: the breakfast rush, the after-school chaos, the goodnight hugs. Amid this whirlwind of activity, emotions ebb and flow, shaping the family dynamics. Empathy, a key component of emotional intelligence, can significantly influence these dynamics.

Let's take the example of a parent and child. The child comes home upset after a bad day at school. Sensing the child's mood, the parent empathetically listens to the child's troubles, offering comfort and understanding. This empathetic response soothes the child and strengthens the bond between parent and child. It sends a powerful message to the child - "Your feelings matter. I'm here for you."

Emotional Regulation in Romantic Relationships

Imagine a couple sitting together yet miles apart, their argument lingering in the air. We've all been there, haven't we? Caught up in the heat of the moment, our emotions flare up, clouding our judgment. Emotional regulation, another facet of emotional intelligence, can be a game-changer.

Returning to the couple, let's say one of them takes a deep breath, deciding to manage their emotional response. They acknowledge their anger but express their feelings calmly and constructively instead of lashing out. This emotionally intelligent response can diffuse the tension, paving the way for a productive conversation and preventing the argument from escalating.

Self-Awareness in Friendships

Picture a group of friends laughing, sharing stories, and simply enjoying each other's company. Friendships like these are built on mutual understanding, shared experiences, and emotional connection. Self-awareness, a cornerstone of emotional intelligence, can play a pivotal role in fostering these connections.

Imagine you're in a group setting, and a friend makes a comment that irks you. Instead of reacting impulsively, you tap into your self-awareness. You recognize your emotional reaction, understand its source, and choose to address it respectfully and considerately. This self-aware response can prevent misunderstandings, enhance communication, and strengthen the bond of friendship.

Our relationships, whether with family, romantic partners, or friends, are the threads that weave the fabric of our lives. Emotional intelligence is the needle that guides these threads, creating a beautiful tapestry of connections, experiences, and memories. Empathy fosters understanding, emotional regulation maintains harmony, and self-awareness nurtures authenticity. By cultivating emotional intelligence, we can enhance our relationships, enriching our lives with deeper connections, mutual respect, and shared growth.

EMOTIONAL INTELLIGENCE IN PROFESSIONAL RELATIONSHIPS

Empathy in Team Collaboration

Imagine you're part of a dynamic project team, each member contributing unique ideas and skills. The team is a melting pot of talent and a minefield of differing opinions and personalities. This is where empathy, a crucial aspect of emotional intelligence, emerges into the spotlight.

Picture a team meeting in which a colleague struggles to articulate an idea. Instead of getting impatient, you tap into your empathy. You try to see the situation from their perspective, understand their difficulty, and offer gentle encouragement. This empathetic approach supports your colleague and fosters a supportive, collaborative atmosphere.

Empathy also plays a pivotal role in appreciating diversity within a team. It helps us understand and respect our colleagues' varying viewpoints, working styles, and cultural backgrounds. This understanding can lead to more inclusive, effective collaboration, strengthening the team's cohesion and productivity.

Emotional Regulation in Leadership

Imagine yourself in a leadership role, guiding a team toward a common goal. The path is often dotted with challenges—tight deadlines, budget constraints, or unexpected roadblocks. Emotional regulation, an essential facet of emotional intelligence, can be your compass during these challenges.

Let's say you're leading a project that's hit a snag. The team is looking to you for direction, their anxiety palpable. While you might be feeling stressed, you choose to regulate your emotions. You maintain a calm demeanor, reassuring your team and focusing on finding solutions. This emotionally balanced response can boost your team's morale, foster trust, and demonstrate your leadership resilience.

Emotional regulation is also crucial in managing feedback. Whether you're delivering constructive criticism or receiving feedback about your leadership style, regulating your emotions can lead to more positive, productive conversations.

Self-Awareness in Conflict Resolution

Finally, let's explore the role of self-awareness in conflict resolution. Conflicts are inevitable in any professional setting. Different opinions and interests can collide, leading to disagreements and tension. Self-awareness, a cornerstone of emotional intelligence, can be valuable in navigating these conflicts.

Imagine a heated argument during a team meeting. Emotions are running high, and the conflict risks escalating. Tapping into your self-awareness, you recognize your rising frustration. But instead of reacting impulsively, you take a moment to understand your emotional response and address the conflict calmly and constructively.

Self-awareness also helps one understand the root causes of conflicts. One can approach disagreements with greater understanding and objectivity by being aware of one's emotional triggers, communication patterns, and conflict style.

Emotional intelligence is like an invisible thread that binds and strengthens professional relationships. Empathy fosters team collaboration, emotional regulation guides leadership, and self-awareness aids conflict resolution. By weaving this thread into our professional interactions, we can build healthier, more effective relationships that enhance our professional success and personal growth.

EFFECTIVE COMMUNICATION TECHNIQUES FOR BETTER RELATIONSHIPS

Active Listening

Think of a time when you've been engaged in a passionate conversation with a friend. The topic is close to your heart, and you share your thoughts, feelings, and experiences. But instead of reciprocating your enthusiasm, your friend keeps interrupting, checking their phone, and barely making eye contact. Frustrating. This is precisely what happens when active listening is absent from a conversation.

Active listening is more than just hearing the words that are spoken. It's about giving your full attention to the speaker, showing interest, and responding in a way that promotes understanding and connection. It's tuning into the subtle nuances of what's being communicated verbally and non-verbally.

You're not just waiting for your turn to speak when you actively listen. You're creating a space for the other person to express themselves freely and showing that you value what they say. This can build trust, reduce misunderstandings, and strengthen relationships.

Non-Verbal Communication

Have you ever talked to someone who constantly avoids eye contact, has their arms crossed, and stands far away? Even if they say all the right things, their body language sends an entirely different message. This highlights the importance of nonverbal communication in our interactions.

Nonverbal cues, such as facial expressions, body language, and tone of voice, often speak louder than words. They can express emotions, indicate attitudes, and complement or contradict what is said verbally.

Knowing your nonverbal communication and accurately interpreting others can enhance your interactions and relationships. It can help you convey your feelings and intentions more effectively and give you valuable insights into what others might think.

Assertive Communication

Have you ever been to a restaurant where you were served the wrong dish? Instead of accepting it or causing a scene, you express your dissatisfaction clearly, respectfully, and firmly. This is an example of assertive communication.

Assertive communication involves openly and honestly expressing one's thoughts, feelings, and needs while also considering the rights, feelings, and needs of others. It's a balanced communication style that promotes respect and understanding, prevents conflicts, and helps build strong relationships.

Assertiveness involves standing up for yourself without being aggressive or passive. It's about setting healthy boundaries, saying no when necessary, and respectfully advocating for your rights. By practicing assertive communication, you can enhance your interpersonal skills, boost your self-confidence, and improve your personal and professional relationships.

Emotional Expression

I'm sure you've watched a movie without sound at some point, maybe even for just a few minutes. You can see the actors' movements, but the story loses its impact without hearing their dialogue or the emotion in their voices. Similarly, emotional expression is crucial in conveying our feelings, needs, and experiences in our relationships.

Emotional expression is about sharing our emotions in a healthy, constructive manner. It's about allowing ourselves to be vulnerable and to express joy, sadness, anger, fear, and love. It's about saying, "I'm excited about this opportunity," "I'm upset about what happened," or "I appreciate your support."

Expressing emotions can enhance our connections with others, build trust, and foster mutual understanding and empathy. It can lead to more authentic and fulfilling relationships. However, it's essential to express our emotions in a way that respects our boundaries and those of others. Emotional intelligence can guide us in navigating this delicate balance, enriching our relationships and emotional well-being.

TRANSFORMING RELATIONSHIPS WITH EMOTIONAL INTELLIGENCE

Emotional Intelligence in Family Relationships

Annika, a mother of two spirited teenagers, is navigating her children's tumultuous teenage years, which are proving challenging. Frequent disagreements and miscommunications were straining their once close-knit bond. Realizing she needed to change her approach, Annika turned to emotional intelligence as a guide, helping her through these "spirited" times.

She began by practicing active listening during her conversations with her children. Instead of offering immediate advice, she would attentively listen to their thoughts and feelings. This simple shift had a profound impact. Her children felt heard and understood, leading to more open and honest conversations.

Annika also made an effort to express her emotions clearly and respectfully. Instead of letting frustrations simmer, she would calmly communicate her feelings. This emotional honesty fostered a more open and understanding family dynamic, reducing conflicts and misunderstandings.

Over time, Annika found that emotional intelligence enhanced her relationship with her children and transformed family dynamics. There was more understanding, better communication, and stronger emotional bonds.

Emotional Intelligence in Workplace Dynamics

Next, let's meet David, a mid-level manager in a fast-paced tech firm. Despite having a competent team, the workplace atmosphere was often tense, marked by stress and misunderstandings. Recognizing the need for change, David decided to weave emotional intelligence into his team dynamics.

David started by cultivating empathy in his interactions with his team members. He strived to understand their perspectives, concerns, and ideas. This empathetic attitude set the stage for a more inclusive and collaborative team environment.

Additionally, David practiced assertive communication, expressing his expectations clearly and respectfully. He also encouraged his team members to do the same. This open line of communication helped clarify misunderstandings, set clear goals, and fostered a sense of mutual respect.

Over time, the impact of emotional intelligence on the team dynamics was evident. There was a noticeable decrease in workplace stress, increased productivity, and an overall improvement in the team's morale.

Emotional Intelligence in Conflict Resolution

Finally, let's look at the story of Mira, an entrepreneur who co-founded a startup with her long-time friend. While their shared vision led to innovative ideas, it also led to frequent conflicts. Mira realized they needed to approach conflicts differently to keep their friendship and business intact.

Mira introduced the practice of self-awareness in their conflict resolution process. She made it a point to identify and understand her emotions during disagreements. This helped her react to conflicts more balanced and less impulsively.

She also emphasized the importance of nonverbal communication. She ensured that her body language and tone of voice were in sync with her words, preventing conflicts from escalating inadvertently.

In time, the influence of emotional intelligence on their conflict resolution was evident. Their disagreements became less heated and more productive, often resulting in creative solutions.

These case studies highlight the transformative power of emotional intelligence in our personal and professional relationships. Whether nurturing family bonds, enhancing workplace dynamics, or resolving conflicts, emotional intelligence will guide us toward healthier, more fulfilling relationships.

Each step improves our relationships and fosters personal growth and emotional well-being. Cultivating emotional intelligence seeds a rich harvest of self-awareness, empathy, and emotional mastery. As we continue to explore empowering ourselves, the next chapter will guide us in applying emotional intelligence in everyday life, transforming challenges into opportunities for growth.

A MAP FOR MODERN LIFE

In the last decade or so, science has discovered a tremendous amount about the role emotions play in our lives. Researchers have found that even more than IQ, your emotional awareness and abilities to handle feelings will determine our success and happiness in all walks of life, including family relationships.

— JOHN GOTTMAN

LIFE CAN FEEL like navigating a complex, ever-changing cityscape in today's fast-paced, technology-driven world. The roads twist and turn, detours appear unexpectedly, and traffic jams challenge our patience. Amid this chaos, emotional intelligence is our GPS—a guidance system that helps us stay on track, reroute when needed, and find the most effective path to our goals.

Just like a GPS doesn't eliminate the obstacles on the road but empowers us to navigate them confidently, emotional intelligence doesn't remove life's challenges. Instead, it equips us with tools to understand our emotions, build stronger relationships, and make intentional decisions aligned with our values. As we explore its practical applications, think of emotional intelligence as the ultimate navigation tool for modern living—helping us manage stress, prioritize effectively, and steer toward a more fulfilling and balanced life.

EMOTIONAL INTELLIGENCE IN PARENTING

Empathy in Parent-Child Communication

As a mother of a toddler and a teenager, Emma's life was filled with laughter, tears, tantrums, and countless "why" questions. She realized that communication with her children was not just about talking but also about empathetic listening.

When her toddler refused to eat his vegetables, instead of asserting her authority, Emma empathetically acknowledged his dislike for the taste. She then explained the benefits of eating vegetables, turning it into a fun game. This empathetic communication made mealtime less of a battle.

When her teenager came home upset after a fight with a friend, Emma didn't rush to offer advice. Instead, she listened empathetically, providing a safe space for her child to express her feelings. This approach helped her teenager feel understood and validated.

Emotional Regulation During Parenting Challenges

Parenting is a joyous journey, but it's not without its challenges. Temper tantrums, sibling fights, and homework struggles can test a parent's patience. For Emma, these were opportunities to practice emotional regulation.

Emma felt her frustration rising when her toddler threw a tantrum in a crowded supermarket. However, she took a deep breath, recognized her emotional response, and responded calmly and firmly, effectively diffusing the situation.

When her teenager broke the curfew, Emma felt angry and worried. Instead of lashing out, she allowed herself to cool down and then expressed her feelings and concerns composed and assertively. This emotionally balanced response opened the door for a constructive conversation about rules and responsibilities.

Building Emotional Resilience in Children

Emma knew that emotional resilience was a valuable skill that would equip her children to handle life's ups and downs. She used her emotional intelligence to foster this resilience in her children.

She encouraged her children to express their emotions, validating their feelings and helping them understand that feeling sad, angry, or scared is okay. She also taught them problem-solving skills, turning setbacks and challenges into learning opportunities.

Over time, Emma noticed a change. Her children were becoming more emotionally expressive, more adept at handling disappointments, and more resilient in facing challenges. As a parent, she raised her children and increased their emotional intelligence.

Emotional intelligence is more than a beneficial skill; it's a map that can guide us through the winding road of everyday life. By cultivating emotional intelligence, we can navigate the landscape of parenting, friendships, loss, and personal growth with great skill and confidence. It's a journey worth embarking on, a journey that enriches not just our lives but also the lives of those around us.

EMOTIONAL INTELLIGENCE IN FRIENDSHIP

Understanding and Respecting Emotional Boundaries

Meet Sofia, a vibrant social butterfly with a wide circle of friends. Her pleasant nature and ability to relate to others have always been her strengths. But she realized that to maintain her friendships, she needed to do more than connect; she needed to respect the emotional boundaries.

Emotional boundaries are invisible lines that define where one person's emotional space begins and another's ends. They are crucial for a healthy friendship, allowing each person to protect their emotional energy, feel safe, and maintain their self-esteem.

Sofia started by acknowledging her friends' emotional boundaries. She learned to read their signals, understand their comfort zones, and respect their need for emotional space. If a friend seemed uncomfortable discussing a particular topic, Sofia would steer the conversation away, respecting their boundary.

This respect for emotional boundaries transformed Sofia's friendships. It fostered mutual respect, trust, and a sense of safety, strengthening the bonds of friendship.

Handling Conflicts with Emotional Intelligence

Even in the best friendships, conflicts are inevitable. Differences of opinion, misunderstandings, or hurt feelings can lead to disputes. Sofia realized handling these conflicts required more than good intentions and emotional intelligence.

Whenever a conflict arose, Sofia used her emotional intelligence. She stepped back, giving herself time to calm down and collect her thoughts. This pause prevented her initial emotional reaction from escalating the conflict.

Next, she would try to understand the other person's perspective, using empathy to guide her. Even if she disagreed, she would validate their feelings, showing that she respected their viewpoint.

Sofia also learned to express her feelings and thoughts assertively, honestly, and respectfully. She would use "I" statements, focusing on expressing her feelings rather than blaming the other person.

These emotionally intelligent strategies transformed Sofia's handling of conflicts. Disagreements were no more prolonged battles to be won but bridges to be mended, strengthening her friendships.

Empathetic Listening in Maintaining Friendships

Friends are the sounding boards of our lives, the ones we turn to share our joys, sorrows, dreams, and fears. Sofia realized that to be a good friend, she needed to be a good listener—but not just any kind of listener, an empathetic listener.

Empathetic listening goes beyond hearing the words that are spoken. It's about tuning into the emotions behind the words, understanding the feelings, and connecting with the person.

Whenever her friends shared their experiences, Sofia would practice empathetic listening. She would give them her undivided attention, show genuine interest, and respond in a way that showed she understood and cared about their feelings.

Empathetic listening deepened Sofia's friendships. Her friends felt heard, understood, and valued, and the power of compassionate listening strengthened and enriched their bonds.

Through these experiences, Sofia learned that emotional intelligence is more than a concept or a skill. It's a way of life, a way of relating to others, a way of nurturing friendships. It's about understanding and respecting emotional boundaries, handling conflicts with empathy and assertiveness, and maintaining friendships through empathetic listening.

Just as a seed requires sunlight, water, and nurturing to thrive, emotional intelligence flourishes when we cultivate self-awareness, empathy, and intentionality in our daily lives. This growth allows us to transform our experiences, interactions, and relationships into opportunities for deeper connection and greater fulfillment. Like a thriving tree, emotional intelligence provides stability in storms, shade in times of overwhelm, and a foundation for continued growth. The more we nurture it, the more we blossom—resilient, grounded, and ready to embrace life's challenges with grace and purpose.

EMOTIONAL INTELLIGENCE IN DEALING WITH LOSS

Emotional Awareness During Grief

Imagine the sudden chill of a winter's night, the quiet solitude accompanying the falling snow. That's what grief can feel like—an unexpected cold that seeps into every corner of your life, leaving you yearning for warmth. Meet Cara, a woman in her late thirties who recently lost her father. Her grief was immense, a wave that threatened to sweep her away. But Cara found solace in her emotional intelligence, particularly her emotional awareness.

Like a fickle storm, grief often brings a whirlwind of emotions — sadness, anger, guilt, fear, even relief. Cara realized that to navigate this storm, she needed to understand its patterns. Her emotional awareness became her weather vane, helping her identify and understand her emotions.

When she felt a surge of anger, she didn't suppress or judge it. Instead, she acknowledged it, understanding that it was a natural part of her grieving process. When guilt gnawed at her, she recognized it, reminding herself it was okay to have regrets. This emotional awareness didn't make the grief disappear, but it provided Cara with a map, guiding her through the stormy terrain of her emotions.

Healthy Emotional Expression in Mourning

In a world that often prioritizes happiness and positivity, expressing grief can feel like swimming against the current. But Cara knew that to heal, she needed to express her grief, not hide it. Healthy emotional expression became her life raft, allowing her to navigate the waves of grief without drowning.

When tears welled in her eyes, Cara let them flow, not holding back. She shared her feelings with loved ones, not worrying about being a burden. She wrote in her journal, pouring her heart onto the pages. This honest, open expression of her emotions was like a pressure valve, releasing the build-up of grief and making it more manageable.

Using Emotional Intelligence for Healing and Acceptance

Healing from a loss isn't about forgetting or moving on; it's about learning to live with the loss and integrating it into your life story. Cara realized that her emotional intelligence, the same beacon that guided her through the storm of grief, could also lead her toward healing and acceptance.

She used her empathy to comfort grieving others, realizing that her loss was part of a shared human experience. This empathy helped others and fostered her healing, reminding her she was not alone in her grief.

Cara also used her self-regulation to manage her grief, allowing herself to feel the pain without letting it consume her. She would take deep breaths when the grief felt overwhelming, practice mindfulness to stay grounded, and engage in self-care activities to nurture her well-being.

Through her emotional intelligence, Cara learned to navigate the landscape of loss. She learned to express her grief healthily, empathize with others, and regulate her emotions. She understood that healing was not about reaching a destination but about the journey—a journey marked by resilience, growth, and a deepened understanding of her emotional world.

Like an unexpected winter, loss can bring a chilling cold into our lives. But with emotional intelligence as our lighthouse, we can learn to endure this cold, navigate the storm of grief, and foster healing and acceptance. We can learn to appreciate the warmth of memories, the comfort of shared sorrow, and the resilience of the human spirit. As we cultivate emotional intelligence, we enhance our ability to deal with loss and enrich our understanding of ourselves and our relationships.

EMOTIONAL INTELLIGENCE IN PERSONAL GROWTH

Self-Awareness for Personal Development

Imagine exploring a brand new city using a compass and navigating many city streets. Self-awareness serves as this compass in personal development, guiding you through the complexities of your inner landscape. Let's meet Liam, a young professional striving to improve his leadership skills.

Liam's work life was bustling with meetings, project deadlines, and team management responsibilities. Amid this busyness, he felt a need to enhance his leadership style. Recognizing that self-awareness was the first step, he began to invest time in introspection, understanding his strengths, weaknesses, and emotional patterns.

Using techniques such as journaling and mindfulness, Liam started examining his reactions to various work situations. He noticed that he often felt anxious during presentations and was occasionally short-tempered with his team during high-stress periods. This level of self-awareness was eye-opening for Liam, providing him with valuable insights into his emotional responses and their impact on his professional life.

Emotional Intelligence in Setting Personal Goals

Armed with a deeper understanding of himself, Liam began setting personal goals for his development. He knew that emotional intelligence could be his ally in this process, assisting him in creating ambitious but emotionally balanced goals.

Liam set a goal to improve his public speaking skills, recognizing that his presentation anxiety hindered his performance. He also resolved to manage stress better to maintain a positive and supportive environment for his team. These goals reflected his emotional intelligence, focusing not just on his professional competencies but also on his emotional responses and relationships.

Emotional Regulation in Personal Transformation

Self-awareness and goal-setting paved the way for Liam's transformation. Emotional regulation played a crucial role in this journey, enabling him to manage his emotional responses effectively and align his behavior with his individual goals.

Liam started practicing deep breathing exercises before presentations to calm his nerves. He also began using positive affirmations to boost his confidence and reduce his anxiety. When work stress escalated, he turned to mindfulness techniques to regain emotional balance and respond calmly and composedly to his team.

Over time, Liam noticed a significant improvement in his leadership skills. His presentations became more confident and impactful, and his team's morale improved due to his balanced and supportive approach during stressful periods.

Through his journey, Liam demonstrated the transformative power of emotional intelligence in personal growth. His story is a testament to how self-awareness, goal-setting, and emotional regulation, the vital components of emotional intelligence, can catalyze personal development and lead to a fulfilling professional life.

As Liam's story illustrates, emotional intelligence is not just a tool for managing emotions or enhancing relationships; it's a catalyst for personal growth. It is like a compass that guides us through our inner landscape, helping us better understand ourselves, set emotionally balanced goals, and transform our lives meaningfully.

Liam's journey is just one of the many ways emotional intelligence can shine its light in our everyday lives. From navigating the challenges of parenting and friendships to dealing with loss and personal growth, emotional intelligence is our guiding lighthouse. Each wave we navigate, and every storm we weather adds to our emotional intelligence, enhancing our understanding, empathy, and resilience.

So, as we close this chapter, let's take a moment to reflect on our journey. Let's celebrate our growth, our learnings, and our resilience. And let's look forward to our continued exploration of emotional intelligence, knowing that with each step we take, we're becoming more emotionally intelligent, understanding, and resilient.

The next chapter will explore how emotional intelligence can be a beacon of light in even the most challenging times. We'll understand how it can help us overcome anxiety, deal with depression, build resilience, and achieve a balanced work-life integration.

YOUR LIFELINE IN ROUGH TIMES

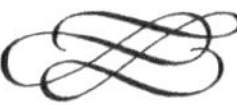

I've learned that people will forget what you said, people will forget what you did, but people will never forget how you made them feel.

— MAYA ANGELOU

THINK of yourself on a roller coaster — that thrill of the climb, the peak's suspense, and the descent's exhilarating rush. Life's ups and downs, twists and turns, can often feel like a roller coaster ride. What if I told you you can navigate this thrilling ride calmly and resiliently? That you can face the plummeting drops of anxiety, the steep climbs of depression, and the sharp turns of life's challenges with greater ease? The secret lies in your power to harness your emotional intelligence. Let's explore how emotional intelligence can be your lifeline in life's twisting and turning roller coaster.

Think of a sturdy bridge stretching across a turbulent river. No matter how fierce the current or strong the winds are, the bridge provides a steady path forward, connecting us to the other side. Emotional intelligence, in many ways, is this bridge. It helps us cross the torrents of fear, navigate the rapids of anxiety, and withstand the storms of life's difficulties with confidence and purpose. By anchoring us in self-awareness, empathy, and resilience, emotional intelligence offers a secure footing, enabling us to move through life's challenges with strength and clarity, always reaching for solid ground.

EMOTIONAL INTELLIGENCE IN OVERCOMING ANXIETY

Recognizing and Understanding Anxiety Triggers

Imagine you're walking through a desert when suddenly, you spot a snake slithering across the dusty path. Your heart pounds, your palms sweat, and a sense of dread overwhelms you. This is anxiety — a natural response to perceived threats or danger. However, when this anxiety becomes frequent, intense, or irrational, it can interfere with your daily life.

Understanding anxiety begins with recognizing its triggers. Triggers are specific situations or events that evoke feelings of anxiety. They can vary widely from person to person. For some, it might be public speaking or social events. For others, it could be work deadlines, health concerns, or relationship issues.

As an emotionally intelligent person, it's crucial to identify your unique anxiety triggers. Self-awareness, a key component of emotional intelligence, can aid in this process. Tuning into your feelings, thoughts, and bodily sensations can give you valuable insights into what triggers your anxiety.

Emotional Self-Regulation Techniques for Anxiety

Now that you've identified your anxiety triggers, the next step is learning to manage your emotional responses to these triggers. This is where emotional self-regulation, another critical aspect of emotional intelligence, comes into play.

Emotional self-regulation involves managing and controlling our emotional reactions, allowing us to respond to our emotions healthier and more adaptive. Here are a few emotional self-regulation techniques that can help manage anxiety:

- Deep Breathing: When anxiety strikes, our breath becomes shallow and rapid. Deep breathing can counter this response, calming the mind and body. Try inhaling deeply, holding your breath for a few seconds, and then exhaling slowly. Repeat this a few times until you feel calmer.
- Progressive Muscle Relaxation: This technique involves tensing and relaxing different muscle groups. It can help relieve physical tension associated with anxiety and promote overall relaxation.
- Mindfulness Meditation: Mindfulness involves focusing on the present moment without judgment. Practicing mindfulness meditation can help you become more aware of your anxiety triggers and manage your emotional responses to them.

Building Emotional Resilience Against Anxiety

While managing anxiety is essential, building emotional resilience can help prevent anxiety from taking hold in the first place. Emotional resilience is the ability to adapt and bounce back in the face of stress or adversity. Here are a few strategies for building emotional resilience against anxiety:

- Emotional Expression: Bottling up your feelings can increase anxiety. Expressing your emotions — whether through talking to a trusted friend, journaling, or creative activities — can help alleviate stress and foster emotional resilience.
- Self-Care: Regular exercise, a healthy diet, adequate sleep, and relaxation activities can boost physical health and emotional resilience and reduce susceptibility to anxiety.
- Positive Relationships: Nurturing positive relationships can provide emotional support and a sense of belonging, which is crucial for emotional resilience.

Remember, overcoming anxiety is not about eliminating all feelings of worry or fear. Instead, it's about understanding your anxiety triggers, managing your emotional responses, and building emotional resilience. With emotional intelligence as your guide, you can navigate the roller coaster of anxiety with greater ease and resilience, making the ride less daunting and more manageable.

OVERCOMING DEPRESSION WITH EMOTIONAL INTELLIGENCE

Emotional Awareness in Identifying Depression

Picture a foggy morning. The world around you is veiled, the landscape obscure, and the path forward unclear. This is what depression can feel like—a dense fog that blurs our joy, drains our energy, and shrouds our world in gloom. To lift depression, we must first understand its presence, density, and impact. This is where emotional awareness, a vital component of emotional intelligence, steps in.

Meet Paula, a successful lawyer in her late forties. From the outside, Paula seemed to have a thriving career, a loving family, and a comfortable life. But inside, she was grappling with a heavy fog of depression. She felt a persistent sadness, a loss of interest in activities she once enjoyed, and a constant fatigue that was hard to shake off.

Paula's journey to recovery began with acknowledging these feelings. She recognized the fog of depression that had settled over her life, understanding its symptoms and acknowledging its impact on her well-being. Her emotional awareness became her first beacon in the dense fog, illuminating the path toward recovery.

Emotional Management Techniques for Depression

Recognizing depression is the first step. Navigating through it requires emotional management, another crucial aspect of emotional intelligence. Emotional management involves understanding, expressing, and regulating emotions healthily and constructively.

Paula decided to reach out for professional help. Her therapist introduced her to a range of emotional management techniques, equipping her with tools to navigate the fog of depression.

One such technique was Cognitive Behavioral Therapy (CBT). CBT helped Paula identify negative thought patterns that were fueling her depression. She learned to challenge these thoughts, replace them with more positive and realistic ones, and manage her feelings more effectively.

Paula also explored mindfulness-based techniques. Mindfulness encouraged her to focus on the present moment, accept her feelings without judgment, and detach from negative thoughts. This practice added a layer of calm to her emotional management toolkit, helping Paula navigate the fog with greater tranquility.

Using Emotional Intelligence for Recovery

Paula embarked on the recovery phase with emotional awareness and management aiding his course. Recovery from depression isn't about snapping back to a "normal" state; it's about gradually lifting the fog, reclaiming your joy, and learning to manage your emotional health.

Paula found that empathy, a key element of emotional intelligence, played a significant role in her recovery. She learned to treat herself with the same compassion she would show a friend going through a similar struggle. This self-empathy softened the harsh self-criticism that often accompanies depression, fostering self-acceptance and self-love.

Another aspect of emotional intelligence that guided Paula's recovery was motivation. Despite the fatigue and lack of interest that depression often brings, Paula pushed herself to engage in activities that she knew would help lift the fog. She resumed her morning runs, spent more time in nature, and reconnected with her love for painting. This intrinsic motivation became a steady force propelling her towards recovery.

Over time, the fog of depression began to lift. The world started regaining its colors, the landscape's clarity, and the path forward its appeal. The journey wasn't easy, and there were days when the fog seemed impenetrable. But with emotional intelligence as his compass, Paula navigated through the dense fog of depression toward a brighter, more straightforward day.

Paula's story illustrates the transformative power of emotional intelligence in overcoming depression. It shows how emotional awareness can help identify depression, how emotional management techniques can navigate through it, and how empathy and motivation can guide recovery. It's a testament to resilience, self-understanding, and the power of emotional intelligence in lifting the fog of depression.

Depression, like a collapsed bridge, left Paula feeling stranded, disconnected, and unsure of how to move forward in her life. She felt the insurmountable gap between where she was and where she wanted to be. But through cultivating emotional intelligence, Paula began rebuilding that bridge, piece by piece, creating a pathway back to connection, clarity, and hope. Emotional intelligence helped her identify the emotions fueling her isolation, understand their origins, and take mindful steps toward recovery.

This reconstructed bridge didn't just get Paula across her current struggles—it became a more robust, resilient structure capable of withstanding future storms. Paula transformed her journey by focusing on self-awareness, empathy, and intentional action. Her bridge became a testament to her strength and a guiding light for others. Paula's story shows us that emotional intelligence offers the tools to rebuild, reconnect, and move toward brighter horizons even when life feels impassable. Each step Paula took strengthened her resilience, illuminated her path and inspired those around her to believe in their ability to overcome challenges.

BUILDING RESILIENCE WITH EMOTIONAL INTELLIGENCE

Understanding the Role of Emotions in Resilience

Let's learn the story of Emily, a woman who faced personal and professional challenges that pushed her to despair. However, Emily was emotionally intelligent and understood emotions' critical role in building resilience.

Emily recognized that each emotion, no matter how uncomfortable or intense, was a natural response to her situation. She allowed herself to feel these emotions—the sadness, the frustration, the fear—without judgment or resistance. She acknowledged, validated, and understood they were temporary, just like the storm.

Accepting her emotions prevented them from overwhelming her. She realized that just as the storm shaped the tree, making it stronger and more resilient, her feelings were shaping her, fostering her resilience and personal growth.

Techniques for Building Emotional Resilience

Being aware of her emotions was just the first step. Emily knew that to build emotional resilience, she needed to manage her emotional responses to adversities effectively.

She began by practicing mindfulness, focusing on the present moment without judgment. This helped her stay grounded amid the chaos, preventing her from being swept away by negative thoughts or worries about the future.

Next, Emily adopted a positive outlook towards her challenges. Instead of seeing them as insurmountable obstacles, she viewed them as opportunities for growth and learning. This shift in perspective reduced her stress and enhanced her emotional well-being.

Emily also cultivated a strong support network — friends and family who provided emotional support, comfort, and encouragement. This social support was like a shield, protecting her against the negative impacts of stress and fostering her emotional resilience.

Real-life Example of Resilience Through Emotional Intelligence

Over time, Emily noticed a transformation. The challenges that once seemed overwhelming now felt manageable. She faced adversities calmly and confidently, bouncing back from setbacks and thriving despite the odds.

One such challenge was when Emily lost her job due to company-wide layoffs. Instead of letting this setback plunge her into despair, she used her emotional intelligence to navigate this challenging time.

She allowed herself to grieve the loss, acknowledging her feelings of disappointment and insecurity. But she also reminded herself that it was okay to feel this way, that her feelings were valid, and that they wouldn't last forever.

Emily then started exploring new job opportunities. She approached this process positively, viewing it as an opportunity to steer her career in a new direction aligned with her interests and values.

Throughout this process, Emily leaned on her support network. She shared her feelings, sought advice, and received encouragement from her friends and family. Their support provided the emotional fuel she needed to keep going.

Today, Emily is employed again and thrives in a role that she loves and better suits her skills and passions. Her story is a testament to the power of emotional intelligence in building resilience. It shows how understanding and managing our emotions, adopting a positive perspective, and leaning on social support can equip us with the strength to weather life's unforeseen challenges.

Emotional intelligence, like the roots of a tree, provides the strength and stability we need to stand tall amid adversities. It guides us through the storm, helps us bend without breaking, and fosters our growth and resilience. So, as we continue to cultivate emotional intelligence, we're not just enhancing our ability to manage emotions or improve relationships; we're also strengthening our resilience and ability to bounce back from adversities and thrive amid life's storms.

USING EMOTIONAL INTELLIGENCE TO ACHIEVE WORK-LIFE BALANCE

Emotional Intelligence in Setting Boundaries

Imagine yourself walking on a tightrope, trying to balance a stack of books in one hand and a cup of coffee in the other. This balancing act often mirrors our struggle to balance work and personal life. One way to steady ourselves in this balancing act is by setting boundaries that emotional intelligence can guide us through.

Meet Kate, a project manager at a bustling digital marketing firm. Kate was often stretched too thin with her demanding job and active social life. She realized she needed to establish clear boundaries to maintain a healthy work-life balance.

Kate started by identifying her limits. She recognized that working late hours was affecting her health and personal relationships. Using her emotional intelligence, she communicated these limits to her team and superiors, ensuring that her work responsibilities didn't take up too much of her time.

This task was difficult, but Kate approached it with assertiveness and empathy. She was firm in her needs yet understanding of her team's needs. Over time, this emotionally intelligent approach to setting boundaries helped Kate achieve a healthier work-life balance, reducing stress and enhancing her overall well-being.

Emotional Management in Workplace Stress

Workplace stress is like a stubborn knot. The more you pull at it without knowing the proper technique, the tighter it gets. Emotional management, a key component of emotional intelligence, can be the technique you need to loosen this knot.

Kate often grappled with workplace stress. Tight deadlines, demanding clients and high-stakes projects were all part of her job. However, Kate managed this stress using her emotional intelligence instead of letting it control her.

She began incorporating mindfulness exercises into her daily routine, taking short breaks to breathe, refocus, and recharge during the day. She also started practicing cognitive reframing, looking at stressful situations from a different, more positive perspective.

Over time, these emotional management strategies helped Kate handle workplace stress more effectively. She was calmer, focused, and more productive, demonstrating that emotional intelligence can be a powerful tool in managing workplace stress.

Emotional Intelligence in Work-Life Integration

Work-life balance is not about drawing a rigid line between work and personal life. It's more about harmoniously integrating the two. This is where emotional intelligence truly shines, helping us blend our professional and personal lives in a way that respects our needs, values, and well-being.

Kate realized that some work responsibilities might require her attention outside regular working hours. Instead of resisting this, she intelligently integrated her work and personal life. She planned her schedule to allow her to attend to important work tasks without sacrificing her time.

For instance, she woke up an hour earlier to review essential reports. This gave her a head start on her workday and freed up her evenings for relaxation and personal activities.

Kate's story is an inspiring example of how emotional intelligence can help achieve work-life balance. By setting boundaries, managing workplace stress, and integrating work and life, Kate created a fulfilling professional life that complemented, rather than conflicted with, her personal life.

The journey to achieving work-life balance is like walking on a tightrope. It requires focus, adjustment, and a deep understanding of our emotions. But with emotional intelligence as our safety net, we can walk this tightrope confidently and gracefully. We can set healthy boundaries, manage workplace stress, and integrate our work and personal lives to enrich our overall quality of life.

So, remember, when you find yourself on this tightrope, look within. Harness your emotional intelligence. It's the balance pole in your hand, the safety net below you, and the confidence within you. With it, you can walk steadily towards a balanced, fulfilling, and happy life.

As we continue exploring emotional intelligence, let's remember its transformative power. It's not just a skill or a concept; it's a way of life that can enhance our relationships, resilience, and well-being.

AN EMOTIONAL INTELLIGENCE PRODUCTIVITY TOOL: THE EISENHOWER MATRIX

IN A WORLD that often pulls us in a dozen directions simultaneously, it's easy to confuse what's truly important with what feels urgent. This struggle can be particularly exhausting for women who are juggling careers, families, relationships, and personal aspirations.

In this chapter, we'll explore a game-changing productivity tool called the Eisenhower Matrix, which is a practical framework to help you take control of your time, energy, and focus. Named after Dwight D. Eisenhower, this method empowers you to distinguish between what requires immediate attention and what truly deserves your long-term effort. You'll learn to categorize tasks, prioritize effectively, and free yourself from the constant rush of "putting out fires." Whether managing work deadlines, balancing personal responsibilities, or seeking more peace in your day-to-day life, this chapter will show you how to create space for what truly matters.

Stephen Covey, renowned author of *The 7 Habits of Highly Effective People,* popularized the concept of prioritizing tasks based on their urgency and importance—a framework rooted in a famous quote attributed to the 34th President of the United States:

> *"What is important is seldom urgent, and what is urgent is seldom important."*

— DWIGHT D. EISENHOWER

Eisenhower's words reflected his disciplined approach to decision-making during his tenure as a five-star general and the 34th President of the United States. Covey transformed this principle into a practical tool now widely known as the Eisenhower Matrix, empowering people to focus on what truly matters while minimizing distractions. For women navigating complex personal and professional responsibilities, the Eisenhower Matrix offers more than a productivity system—it's a gateway to practicing emotional intelligence by making intentional choices that align with their values and emotions. This chapter explores how the Eisenhower Matrix and emotional intelligence intersect, equipping women to manage their time and emotions confidently and clearly.

Emotional intelligence is often described as the ability to understand and manage emotions effectively in ourselves and others. Making intentional, value-driven decisions is one of the most practical ways to incorporate emotional intelligence into our daily lives. In this chapter, we'll explore how the Eisenhower Matrix—a time-management tool popularized by former U.S. President Dwight D. Eisenhower—can serve as a vital framework for enhancing emotional intelligence.

The Eisenhower Matrix helps us organize tasks based on urgency and importance, offering a structured way to prioritize. While the matrix is primarily a productivity tool, it has more profound implications for emotional intelligence. Combining the Eisenhower Matrix's clarity with EI skills allows women to navigate life's demands with greater focus, resilience, and peace of mind.

UNDERSTANDING THE EISENHOWER MATRIX

The Eisenhower Matrix divides tasks into four quadrants. Imagine four squares of the same size, with two squares on top and two on the bottom.

Covey's modern Eisenhower Matrix quadrants are laid out from upper left to lower right, with quadrants in numerical order.

Quadrant 1: Urgent and Important (Do)

Tasks in this quadrant require immediate attention and, if not addressed, can have significant consequences. Examples include meeting critical deadlines, handling crises, and attending to pressing personal matters.

Quadrant 2: Not Urgent but Important (Decide)

This is the quadrant for long-term planning and relationship building. It includes strategic goal-setting, skill development, and self-care practices.

Quadrant 3: Urgent but Not Important (Delegate)

These tasks demand immediate attention but don't contribute significantly to personal goals. Examples include routine administrative work or interruptions that others could handle.

Quadrant 4: Neither Urgent nor Important (Delete)

Often considered time-wasters, these activities add little value to your life. Examples include excessive social media scrolling or unnecessary meetings.

The Eisenhower Matrix is more than a task management method—it's a tool for aligning actions with values. Emotional intelligence enhances the matrix's application by providing the self-awareness, empathy, and decision-making skills to prioritize effectively. Let's break down how EI intersects with the four quadrants.

FURTHER EXPLANATION OF QUADRANTS

Here is an additional explanation of the related quadrants and how they relate to what we've already learned in this book.

Quadrant 1: Urgent and Important (Emotional Resilience in Action)

Stress and pressure often run high when handling urgent and essential tasks. Emotional intelligence is critical to maintaining composure, focusing on solutions, and managing emotional responses.

Example: Imagine a working mother managing a family emergency while preparing for a significant work presentation. Without emotional regulation, the stress could feel overwhelming, leading to burnout or errors.

How emotional intelligence helps:

- Self-awareness: Early recognition of signs of stress—racing thoughts, irritability, or fatigue—helps you respond rather than react.
- Self-regulation: Techniques such as deep breathing or mindfulness exercises can prevent emotional escalation and help you stay focused.
- Empathy: Understanding the emotions of others involved, such as a distressed child or an anxious colleague, enables you to provide reassurance and maintain healthy communication.

Quadrant 2: Not Urgent but Important (Building Emotional Intelligence Through Intentionality)

Quadrant 2 is where growth and balance occur. Activities like self-care, learning, and nurturing relationships reside here. Emotional intelligence encourages us to prioritize this quadrant because it aligns with long-term well-being and fulfillment.

Example: Consider a woman who wants to improve her health but struggles to make time for exercise amid daily responsibilities. Without prioritizing it in Quadrant 2, she risks burnout or health issues, which may eventually spill into Quadrant 1.

How emotional intelligence helps:

- Prioritization: Emotional intelligence allows you to assess what truly matters to you—health, personal growth, or relationships—and allocate time accordingly.
- Empathy Toward Self: Recognizing that self-care is not selfish but essential helps women overcome societal guilt or pressure to "do it all."
- Strategic Vision: Goal-setting with emotional intelligence ensures alignment with core values, preventing regret from neglecting what's important.

Quadrant 3: Urgent but Not Important (Delegation With Confidence)

Many women struggle with delegation due to a desire to maintain control or fear of disappointing others. Tasks in Quadrant 3 often drain energy without contributing to personal or professional goals. Emotional intelligence equips women to recognize these patterns and act differently.

Example: Picture a team leader who spends hours addressing minor team requests instead of focusing on strategic planning. Without delegation, she risks stagnation in her role.

How emotional intelligence helps:

- Social Awareness: Understanding the strengths and capabilities of others enables effective delegation.
- Assertive Communication: EI helps you say "no" or set boundaries without damaging relationships. For example, instead of taking on extra work, you might say, "I'd love to

help, but I need to focus on [priority task]. Could someone else assist with this?"

- Building Trust: Delegating tasks fosters a sense of empowerment among team members, improving overall efficiency and morale.

Quadrant 4: Neither Urgent nor Important (Emotional Intelligence for Letting Go)

Tasks in Quadrant 4 often represent procrastination or escapism. Emotional intelligence helps us identify these distractions and consciously choose to eliminate them.

An example is a person who spends hours scrolling social media, avoiding an uncomfortable but necessary conversation with a friend or partner.

How emotional intelligence helps:

- Self-Awareness: Recognizing when avoidance behaviors stem from stress or fear allows you to address the root cause.
- Impulse Control: EI strengthens the ability to resist distractions and focus on what truly matters.
- Purpose Alignment: Eliminating time-wasters creates space for Quadrant 2 activities that align with your values and goals.

PRACTICAL APPLICATIONS OF THE EISENHOWER MATRIX WITH EMOTIONAL INTELLIGENCE

To integrate the Eisenhower Matrix into your life using emotional intelligence, consider the following steps:

Step 1: Reflect on Your Values and Priorities

Emotional intelligence begins with self-awareness. Spend time identifying your core values, such as family, health, career, or creativity. Use these as a compass to evaluate tasks and ensure your actions align with your priorities.

Exercise:

- List your top five values.
- Write down how your daily activities support or conflict with these values.

Step 2: Create Your Matrix

At the start of each week, categorize tasks into the four quadrants. Be honest about their urgency and importance.

Quadrant Identifying Tip: Color-code tasks (e.g., red for Quadrant 1, green for Quadrant 2, etc.) to visualize your priorities.

Step 3: Use Emotional Intelligence to Navigate Challenges

If you have an overload in Quadrant 1:

- Acknowledge feelings of stress and use emotional regulation techniques to stay calm and productive.
- Seek support from others when needed, practicing assertiveness and empathy.

Maximizing Quadrant 2 Activities:

- Schedule time for Quadrant 2 tasks daily, even if only for 15 minutes.
- Remind yourself of the long-term benefits of prioritizing these activities, such as stronger relationships or improved health.

Delegating Quadrant 3 Tasks:

- Identify people who can handle specific tasks and communicate clearly.
- Practice letting go of perfectionism; done is better than perfect.

Eliminating Quadrant 4 Distractions:

- Use technology to your advantage, such as apps that block social media during work hours.
- Reflect on the emotional triggers behind procrastination and address them proactively.

Step 4: Regularly Reassess Your Matrix

Life is dynamic, and priorities shift. Review your matrix weekly to ensure it reflects your current goals and emotional state.

Reflection Questions:

- Are Quadrant 1 tasks dominating your time? If so, what can you plan in Quadrant 2 to prevent future crises?
- Are you dedicating enough time to activities that bring joy and fulfillment?

Applying the Eisenhower Matrix to Emotional Intelligence

Let's meet Ana. Ana is a busy entrepreneur and mother of two. She often feels pulled in multiple directions, with little time for herself. IF Ana were to utilize the Eisenhower Matrix, her quadrants might look something like this:

- Quadrant 1: Meeting deadlines for client projects and managing her children's school emergencies.
- Quadrant 2: Attending yoga classes, spending quality time with her children, and planning her business expansion.

- Quadrant 3: Answering non-urgent emails and handling minor team conflicts.
- Quadrant 4: Watching TV for hours after a stressful day.

By combining the Eisenhower Matrix with emotional intelligence:

- Ana used self-awareness to realize she was neglecting Quadrant 2 tasks.
- She practiced self-regulation to stop overreacting to Quadrant 1 crises.
- She employed delegation to pass Quadrant 3 tasks to her assistant.
- Finally, Ana eliminated Quadrant 4 distractions, replacing them with mindful relaxation activities.

After six months, Ana reported feeling more balanced, energized, and aligned with her goals.

What have we learned?

The Eisenhower Matrix is more than a productivity tool; it's a framework for intentional living. Combined with emotional intelligence, it helps women align their actions with their values, navigate stress with resilience, and create space for what truly matters.

By integrating the principles of emotional intelligence into the Eisenhower Matrix, women can transform how they approach their tasks and emotions. This synergy allows for a more balanced life where priorities are clear, stress is manageable, and time is spent meaningfully.

As you move forward, consider regularly adopting the Eisenhower Matrix. Pair it with self-reflection, empathy, and mindful decision-making. Doing so will enhance your emotional intelligence and help you create a life that reflects your values, ambitions, and well-being.

The journey is about more than getting things done—it's about choosing the right things to do and doing them with intention and grace.

The next chapter examines case studies of women who utilize this book's daily techniques and exercises. See if you can recognize the practical, emotional intelligence methods being displayed.

EMOTIONAL INTELLIGENCE CASE STUDIES

LIFE OFTEN FEELS like a juggling act. Managing workplace demands, nurturing personal relationships, and stepping into leadership roles can leave even the strongest of us feeling stretched thin. Add the weight of personal setbacks or the daily grind of stress, and it's easy to feel overwhelmed. But here's the good news: emotional intelligence isn't just a buzzword—it's a powerful tool that can transform how we navigate these challenges.

In this chapter, you'll meet five remarkable women, each facing their struggles. Through case studies, we'll explore how emotional intelligence helped one woman tackle workplace conflicts, another balance the complexities of personal relationships, and a leader inspire and empower her team. We'll also dive into stories of resilience—overcoming personal setbacks and managing stress without losing sight of self-care.

These stories aren't just inspiring—they're practical. Each case study reveals strategies and insights you can apply in your own life. By the end of this chapter, you'll have real-world examples of how emotional intelligence can help you take control, find balance, and turn challenges into opportunities for growth. Let's explore how these lessons bring clarity, confidence, and calm into your world.

CASE STUDY: NAVIGATING WORKPLACE CHALLENGES

Emma's Story: A Test of Leadership and Empathy

Emma had always been a diligent and high-achieving professional. As a mid-level manager at a tech company, she was known for her technical expertise and ability to meet deadlines. However, she often struggled to connect emotionally with her team. This became a glaring issue during a high-stakes project when tensions flared among team members, threatening the project's success.

The project involved tight deadlines, competing priorities, and diverse employees with varying work styles. Emma noticed that Sarah, a junior team member, consistently withdrew from discussions. Meanwhile, Chris, another team member, grew increasingly vocal, often interrupting others during meetings. The friction between the two began to affect team morale and productivity.

Emma initially tried to focus on the technical aspects of the project, assuming that staying task-oriented would resolve the conflict. However, she soon realized that ignoring the emotional undercurrents only worsened the situation. She decided to take a step back and apply emotional intelligence to address the root causes of the tension.

APPLYING EMOTIONAL INTELLIGENCE

Self-Awareness

Emma started by reflecting on her own emotions. She acknowledged feeling frustrated and overwhelmed, which influenced her interactions. Recognizing this allowed her to approach the situation more calmly and objectively.

Empathy

Emma scheduled one-on-one meetings with Sarah and Chris to understand their perspectives. Sarah revealed that she felt dismissed during meetings, which led to her withdrawal. Chris admitted that he often interrupted out of enthusiasm but hadn't realized it came across as dominating.

Social Awareness

Observing team dynamics, Emma noticed that other members were also affected by the tension but were reluctant to speak up. She realized that addressing the issue openly would benefit the entire team.

Relationship Management

Emma facilitated a team meeting focused on improving communication. She encouraged everyone to share their concerns constructively, validated their feelings using active listening, and set clear expectations for respectful interactions.

Outcome

Through her emotionally intelligent approach, Emma was able to foster a healthier team environment. The project was completed successfully, and the team emerged more robust, with a newfound appreciation for open communication and mutual respect.

Key Takeaways:

- Self-awareness helps leaders manage their own emotions and approach conflicts calmly.
- Empathy and active listening are crucial for understanding others' perspectives.
- Setting clear boundaries and expectations enhances team dynamics and productivity.

CASE STUDY: BALANCING PERSONAL RELATIONSHIPS

Cara's Story: The Art of Setting Boundaries

Cara had always been the friend everyone relied on. Whether it was providing emotional support, helping with last-minute favors, or listening to long rants late at night, she prided herself on being dependable. However, this role often left her feeling drained and unappreciated. One friendship, particularly with her college roommate Maya, had become incredibly taxing.

Maya was going through a tough time in her career and personal life. While Cara empathized with her struggles, she often spent hours listening to Maya's problems, with little opportunity to share her thoughts. This imbalance started to take a toll on Cara's mental health and her ability to focus on her work and other relationships.

One evening, after a particularly draining phone call, Cara realized something had to change. She needed to find a way to support Maya without compromising her well-being. Emotional intelligence became her guiding tool.

APPLYING EMOTIONAL INTELLIGENCE

Self-Awareness

Cara began by identifying her feelings of frustration and exhaustion. She recognized that her tendency to avoid conflict and always say "yes" was a major contributor to the imbalance in the relationship.

Emotional Regulation

Instead of reacting out of frustration, Cara approached the situation thoughtfully. She practiced deep breathing before conversations with Maya and reminded herself that setting boundaries was not an act of selfishness but self-care.

Empathy

Cara considered Maya's perspective. She realized that Maya's reliance on her wasn't malicious but came from a place of vulnerability. Understanding this allowed Cara to approach the conversation with compassion rather than resentment.

Effective Communication

During their following conversation, Cara gently but firmly expressed her feelings. She told Maya, "I value our friendship, and I want to support you. But sometimes, I feel overwhelmed and need time for myself. I hope you understand." She also encouraged Maya to explore other sources of support, such as therapy or mutual friends.

Outcome

While Maya initially seemed taken aback, she eventually appreciated Cara's honesty. Their friendship became more balanced as Cara learned to set boundaries, and Maya sought other ways to cope with her challenges. Cara felt empowered and more in control of her time and energy.

Key Takeaways

- Recognizing emotional exhaustion is the first step toward addressing imbalances in relationships.
- Empathy allows difficult conversations to be approached with kindness and understanding.
- Setting boundaries strengthens relationships by ensuring they remain mutually supportive.

CASE STUDY: THRIVING AS A LEADER

Louise's Story: Transformational Leadership Through Emotional Resilience

Louise headed a marketing team at a rapidly growing startup. Known for her creativity and strategic thinking, she was well-respected among her peers. However, when the company underwent a significant restructuring, Louise faced one of the biggest challenges of her career.

Her team was reduced by half, and the remaining members were overwhelmed with increased workloads. Morale was at an all-time low, and Louise noticed rising frustration and burnout among her team. She knew she needed to step up as a leader but also felt the weight of her stress and doubts.

Louise focused on emotional intelligence as a leadership strategy to guide her team through this turbulent time.

How Louise applied emotional intelligence:

Self-Awareness

Louise took time to reflect on her own emotions. She acknowledged her feelings of anxiety and fear of failure but recognized that projecting confidence and empathy was crucial for her team's stability.

Social Awareness

By paying close attention to her team's behavior, Louise noticed signs of burnout, such as decreased productivity and a lack of engagement during meetings. She empathized with their challenges and validated

Emotional Regulation

To manage her stress, Louise incorporated mindfulness practices into her routine. She also sought support from a mentor, which helped her maintain a clear perspective.

Relationship Management

Louise organized a team meeting to address concerns openly. She encouraged everyone to share their challenges and proposed practical solutions, such as redistributing workloads and introducing flexible deadlines. She regularly checked in with her team individually to provide personalized support.

Inspiring Others

Louise shared her vision for how the team could emerge stronger despite the setbacks. By highlighting their collective strengths and celebrating small wins, she reignited their sense of purpose.

Outcome

Louise's emotionally intelligent leadership transformed the team's dynamic. They felt heard, valued, and motivated to rise to the challenge. The team completed several key projects, and Louise was recognized by senior management for her exceptional leadership during a difficult time.

Key Takeaways

- Leaders must manage their own emotions to guide their teams effectively.
- Empathy and open communication foster trust and collaboration.
- Recognizing and celebrating achievements boosts team morale and resilience.

CASE STUDY: OVERCOMING PERSONAL SETBACKS

Maria's Story: Rebuilding Confidence After Divorce

Maria's world turned upside down when her 15-year marriage ended in divorce. As a stay-at-home mother, she had dedicated most of her adult life to her family. Now, faced with the prospect of starting over, Maria felt lost and overwhelmed by feelings of inadequacy and fear.

Determined to rebuild her life, Maria focused on developing her emotional intelligence to navigate this challenging period.

Which tools did Maria apply to emotional intelligence?

Self-Awareness

Maria began journaling to explore her emotions and identify recurring patterns of self-doubt. She realized that much of her fear stemmed from comparing herself to others and internalizing societal expectations.

Self-Compassion

Instead of criticizing herself for the past, Maria practiced self-compassion. She reminded herself that setbacks are a natural part of life and an opportunity for growth.

Empathy

Maria sought support from a local divorce support group. Hearing others' stories helped her realize she wasn't alone in her struggles, fostering a sense of connection and understanding.

Goal Setting

Maria created a list of personal and professional goals, starting with small, manageable steps. She enrolled in a community college course to update her skills and explored part-time job opportunities.

Resilience

Whenever she faced setbacks, Maria used mindfulness techniques to stay grounded and focused on her long-term vision. She also celebrated small milestones, such as completing her first college assignment, to boost her confidence.

Outcome

Over time, Maria regained her sense of identity and independence. She found a fulfilling job, strengthened her relationships with her children, and even discovered new hobbies that brought her joy. Through emotional intelligence, Maria overcame her setbacks and built a proud life.

Key Takeaways

- Self-awareness and self-compassion are essential for healing after personal setbacks.
- Seeking support fosters resilience and provides valuable perspective.
- Setting achievable goals helps rebuild confidence and a sense of purpose.

CASE STUDY: HANDLING EVERYDAY STRESS

Alisha's Story: Finding Balance as an Entrepreneur

Alisha was a passionate entrepreneur who juggled multiple roles. Between managing her growing business, caring for her family, and maintaining her personal life, she often felt like there weren't enough hours in the day. The constant stress began affecting her health and relationships, leaving her feeling exhausted and irritable.

Determined to find a healthier balance, Alisha turned to emotional intelligence to manage her stress effectively.

How Alisha applied emotional intelligence to her situation described above:

Self-Awareness

Alisha kept a stress journal to identify her triggers. She realized that her perfectionism and tendency to overcommit significantly contributed to her stress.

Emotional Regulation

Alisha practiced deep breathing and mindfulness meditation to calm her mind during high-stress moments. She also learned to say "no" to non-essential tasks without guilt.

Social Awareness

Alisha communicated openly with her family and business team about her challenges. Their support and understanding lightened her emotional load.

Time Management

Alisha prioritized her tasks using the Eisenhower Matrix, focusing on what was urgent and essential. She also delegated responsibilities to her team, trusting them to handle tasks independently.

Self-Care

Alisha carved out time for activities that rejuvenated her, such as yoga and reading. This helped her recharge and approach her responsibilities with renewed energy.

Outcome

By applying emotional intelligence, Alisha transformed her approach to stress. She achieved a healthier work-life balance, improved her relationships, and continued to grow her business without compromising her well-being.

Key Takeaways

- Identifying stress triggers is the first step to managing them effectively.
- Open communication and delegation reduce emotional and logistical burdens.
- Prioritizing self-care enhances productivity and overall well-being.

As you've read throughout this book, emotional intelligence is not just a concept; it's a transformative tool that empowers women to navigate the complexities of their personal and professional lives with grace, resilience, and authenticity. The case studies in this chapter show how emotional intelligence manifests in real-life situations, offering practical solutions to women's daily challenges.

Reflecting on the Lessons

Each example and case study in this book highlights a core aspect of emotional intelligence—self-awareness, self-regulation, empathy, social awareness, and relationship management. These components are not separate skills but interwoven qualities that complement and strengthen each other. Let's break down some of the methods used in the case studies we've read about in this chapter.

- **Self-awareness:** Whether Emma recognizes her frustration, Cara understands her emotional exhaustion, or Alisha identifies her stress triggers, self-awareness is the foundation for change. Looking inward and acknowledging our emotions without judgment enables us to take purposeful action.
- **Self-Regulation:** Emotional intelligence teaches us to manage our emotions rather than letting them control us. Louise used self-regulation to lead her team confidently, while Maria used mindfulness to rebuild her life after divorce. These examples remind us that self-regulation isn't about suppressing emotions but responding constructively.
- **Empathy:** Empathy allows us to see the world through others' eyes, fostering deeper connections and understanding. Cara's ability to empathize with Maya's struggles strengthened their friendship, while Louise's empathy helped her team overcome adversity.
- **Social Awareness and Relationship Management:** These skills help women nurture fulfilling and sustainable relationships, whether by building trust in the workplace or creating healthy boundaries in friendships.

THE UNIQUE POWER OF WOMEN IN EMOTIONAL INTELLIGENCE

Women are naturally inclined toward empathy and relationship-building, giving them a unique advantage in cultivating emotional intelligence. However, societal pressures, gender norms, and the demands of balancing multiple roles can make it challenging to prioritize emotional well-being.

By embracing emotional intelligence, women can reclaim their power and create lives that reflect their values, aspirations, and individuality. They can become not just problem-solvers but also empathetic leaders, supportive friends, and resilient individuals who inspire others.

To continue your journey of developing emotional intelligence, here are some additional practical tools and strategies:

- **Journaling:** Writing about your emotions can help you identify patterns and triggers, fostering self-awareness.
- **Mindfulness Practices:** Techniques like meditation, deep breathing, and yoga can improve emotional regulation and reduce stress.
- **Active Listening:** Practice listening without interrupting or forming judgments. This builds empathy and strengthens relationships.
- **Feedback Seeking:** Regularly ask for feedback from trusted friends, colleagues, or mentors to understand how your emotions and behaviors affect others.
- **Professional Development:** Attend workshops or read books on emotional intelligence to deepen your understanding and application of EI skills.

A Call to Action

As we approach the end of this chapter, take a moment to reflect on your journey with emotional intelligence.

Consider these questions:

- How do you typically respond to challenges or conflicts?
- What steps can you take to understand and manage your emotions better?

- In what areas of your life can emotional intelligence make the most significant impact?

By looking inward and using emotional intelligence to seek the answers to the questions above, you have learned, understood, and applied the material presented in this book.

As we leave this chapter, I will remind you that your emotional intelligence may look drastically different from another person's, and that's entirely acceptable. Emotional Intelligence is not mirrored from person to person; each individual's emotional intelligence comes from within. When you are regularly mindful of your emotional intelligence, the world around you will seem happier and less mentally taxing.

FINAL THOUGHTS

WE HAVE COME to the end of the book, my friend, and I humbly appreciate your decision to trust my book to educate, illuminate, and guide you on your emotional intelligence journey.

Remember, emotional intelligence is a lifelong journey. It's not about achieving perfection but about continual growth and self-discovery. Each small step you take toward understanding yourself and others will have a ripple effect, enriching your life and the lives of those around you.

The example stories of each woman in the book and the few men remind us that emotional intelligence is practical and powerful. It enables women to turn obstacles into opportunities, nurture meaningful relationships, and lead authentically and courageously. As you move forward, let these stories inspire you to embrace your emotional intelligence and unleash your full potential.

I'll leave you with some final encouragement. The emotional intelligence journey begins with one single step: understanding the emotions that shape your world and choosing to act with intention and empathy. Developing emotional intelligence is a lifelong process;

the most essential step is consistent practice. Start small, build habits, and allow yourself grace along the way. By investing in your emotional intelligence, you're not only enriching your own life but also creating a positive ripple effect in your relationships, career, and community.

Dedication and practice make the emotional growth journey a rewarding and empowering experience. With emotional intelligence as your guide, there is no limit to what you can achieve.

With Gratitude,

Akari

GLOSSARY OF EMOTIONAL INTELLIGENCE TERMS

A

Active Listening: Fully concentrating, understanding, responding, and remembering what is said in a conversation.

Authenticity: Being genuine and honest in your emotional expressions and interactions.

B

Body Language: Nonverbal cues that communicate emotions and intentions.

C

Cognitive Reframing: Changing negative or unhelpful thought patterns into positive or constructive ones.

Compassion Fatigue: Emotional exhaustion from consistently caring for others' emotional needs.

Conflict Resolution: The process of resolving a dispute or disagreement constructively and empathetically.

D

Distress Tolerance: The ability to endure and manage emotional discomfort.

E

Emotion Coaching: Guiding someone, especially children, to understand and regulate their emotions.

Emotion-Focused Coping: Strategies aimed at managing emotions in response to stress.

Emotional Adaptability: The ability to adjust emotional responses based on new information or circumstances.

Emotional Agility: The ability to navigate and respond to emotions healthily and productively.

Emotional Amplification: Heightening emotions through internal or external factors.

Emotional Amplification: Heightening emotions through internal or external factors.

Emotional Anchoring: Using positive memories or thoughts to stabilize emotions in difficult times.

Emotional Attunement: Being in sync with your or others' emotional states.

Emotional Boundaries: Limits that define how much emotional energy you give or accept from others.

Emotional Burnout: Exhaustion caused by prolonged exposure to emotional stress.

Emotional Calibration: Aligning your emotional responses with the demands of the situation.

Emotional Clarity: The ability to understand and define your emotions accurately.

Emotional Congruence: Alignment between one's internal emotions and external expressions.

Emotional Contagion: The phenomenon of emotions spreading from one person to another.

Emotional Dependency: Excessive reliance on others to regulate one's emotions.

Emotional Drainage: Feelings of exhaustion caused by excessive emotional effort or interactions.

Emotional Feedback: Responses or reactions to others that reflect your emotions or perceptions.

Emotional Flexibility: The capacity to adapt emotional responses to changing circumstances.

Emotional Harmony: Achieving a balanced and positive emotional state.

Emotional Independence: The ability to regulate emotions without relying on external validation.

Emotional Intelligence (EI): The ability to recognize, understand, and manage our own emotions and to influence the feelings of others.

Emotional Intelligence Quotient (EQ): A measure of an individual's emotional intelligence.

Emotional Intelligence Training: Programs designed to enhance understanding and application of emotional intelligence skills.

Emotional Literacy: The ability to effectively identify, understand, and express emotions.

Emotional Plasticity: The ability to change and grow emotionally over time.

Emotional Projection: Attributing one's own emotions to someone else.

Emotional Regulation: Managing and adjusting your emotional responses to situations or stimuli.

Emotional Resilience: Maintaining or regaining emotional equilibrium during stressful situations.

Emotional Safety: A state where individuals feel secure enough to express emotions without fear of judgment.

Emotional Suppression: The act of consciously inhibiting the expression of emotions.

Emotional Triggers: Situations or events that elicit strong emotional reactions.

Emotional Validation: Acknowledging and accepting another person's emotions as valid and understandable.

Empathic Accuracy: The ability to accurately perceive another person's emotions or intentions.

Empathic Listening: Listening to understand the speaker's emotions and perspective.

Empathy: The ability to understand and share the feelings of another person.

G

Gratitude Practice: Regularly reflecting on and expressing thanks that fosters positive emotional states.

I

Impulse Control: The ability to resist urges or impulses that may be inappropriate or counterproductive.

Interpersonal Effectiveness: The ability to navigate social situations and relationships skillfully and tactfully.

M

Mindfulness: The practice of being fully present and aware of one's emotions and surroundings.

Motivation: The drive to achieve goals for personal reasons rather than external rewards.

N

Nonverbal Communication: The transmission of messages or emotions without words, including gestures, facial expressions, and tone of voice.

O

Optimism: Maintaining a positive outlook even when faced with challenges.

P

Personal Accountability: Taking responsibility for your emotions, actions, and consequences.

R

Relational Intelligence: The capacity to manage and nurture interpersonal relationships effectively.

Resilience: The ability to bounce back from setbacks, challenges, or adversity.

S

Self-Awareness: The capacity to recognize and understand your emotions, thoughts, and behaviors.

Self-Compassion: Treating oneself with kindness and understanding during failure or difficulty.

Self-Reflection: Examining one's thoughts, emotions, and behaviors to gain insight.

Self-Regulation: The ability to control or redirect disruptive emotions and impulses and adapt to changing circumstances.

Social Awareness: The capacity to understand and empathize with the emotions and needs of others.

Social Capital: The networks and relationships built through emotional and social skills.

Social Skills: The ability to build and manage healthy interpersonal relationships effectively.

T

Trustworthiness: Demonstrating integrity and honesty in your interactions with others.

V

Vulnerability: The willingness to express emotions openly, even when it involves risk or uncertainty.

ABOUT THE AUTHOR

Akari Yin is the granddaughter of Chinese immigrants who settled in the United States in the late 20th century. Her grandparents came seeking better opportunities, bringing rich traditions and values that shaped her worldview. Growing up in a bicultural household, she learned to balance Eastern philosophies of harmony and mindfulness with Western ideals of progress and individuality.

With a background in psychology and training in holistic healing modalities such as meditation, acupuncture, and "Shen" (which is attributed to the heart, mind, and soul, representing a holistic connection between the physical, mental, and spiritual aspects of a person), Akari integrates these practices with modern emotional intelligence principles. Akari believes true empowerment comes from understanding the connection between mind, body, and spirit spirit.

Akari Yin's work focuses on helping women harness emotional intelligence to heal, grow, and thrive. Through workshops, one-on-one coaching, and her writing, she empowers women to build resilience, navigate life's challenges with grace, and create meaningful connections. Her approach blends scientific research with ancient wisdom, making emotional intelligence accessible and transformative for all.

REFERENCES

Ahmad, Usman. "Unlocking Personal Growth: The Power of Emotional Intelligence." *Medium*, 5 July 2023, medium.com/@usmanahmadsgd/unlocking-personal-growth-the-power-of-emotional-intelligence-f696a52cdc7e. Accessed 1 Dec. 2024.

Asana. "The Eisenhower Matrix: How to Prioritize Your To-Do List." *Asana*, 29 Jan. 2024, asana.com/resources/eisenhower-matrix. Accessed 19 Aug. 2024.

Baer, Mark. "Empathy Is the Key to Conflict Resolution or Management." *Psychology Today*, 28 Feb. 2017, www.psychologytoday.com/us/blog/empathy-and-relationships/201702/empathy-is-the-key-conflict-resolution-or-management. Accessed 20 Aug. 2024.

Birt, Jamie. "The Importance of Emotional Intelligence in the Workplace." *Indeed Career Guide*, 12 Dec. 2019, www.indeed.com/career-advice/career-development/emotional-intelligence-importance. Accessed 6 Sept. 2023.

Bluesoft. "Manage the Anxiety with Emotional Intelligence." *Www.brightconcept-Consulting.com*, 9 Apr. 2020, www.brightconcept-consulting.com/en/blog/emotional-intelligence/closing-the-door-to-anxiety-the-role-of-emotional-intelligence-in-a-crisis. Accessed 26 Aug. 2024.

Cherry, Kendra. "IQ vs. EQ: Which One Is More Important?" *Verywell Mind*, 7 Dec. 2022, www.verywellmind.com/iq-or-eq-which-one-is-more-important-2795287. Accessed 14 Oct. 2023.

Collado-Soler, Rocio, et al. "Emotional Intelligence and Resilience Outcomes in Adolescent Period, Is Knowledge Really Strength?" *Psychology Research and Behavior Management*, vol. Volume 16, Apr. 2023, pp. 1365–1378, https://doi.org/10.2147/prbm.s383296.

Compare, Angelo, et al. "Emotional Regulation and Depression: A Potential Mediator between Heart and Mind." *Cardiovascular Psychiatry and Neurology*, vol. 2014, no. 324374, 2014, pp. 1–10, pmc.ncbi.nlm.nih.gov/articles/PMC4090567/, https://doi.org/10.1155/2014/324374. Accessed 16 July 2024.

Edis, Noah. "30 Best Quotes about Emotional Intelligence." *ThinkPsych*, 7 Feb. 2024, thinkpsych.com/blogs/posts/30-best-quotes-about-emotional-intelligence? Accessed 8 June 2024.

"Emotional Intelligence and Its Role in Relationships." *Intelligent Change*, www.intelligentchange.com/blogs/read/emotional-intelligence-and-its-role-in-relationships. Accessed 15 Aug. 2024.

Espy, Leigh. "5 Ways Emotional Intelligence Builds Trust through Communication." *PMWorld 360 Magazine - the Project Manager Magazine*, PMWorld 360 Magazine, 19 July 2022, www.pmworld360.com/5-ways-emotional-intelligence-builds-trust-through-communication/. Accessed 14 Mar. 2024.

Farrahi, Hassan, et al. "Emotional Intelligence and Its Relationship with General Health among the Students of University of Guilan, Iran." *Iranian Journal of Psychiatry and Behavioral Sciences*, vol. 9, no. 3, 23 Sept. 2015, www.ncbi.nlm.nih.gov/pmc/articles/PMC4644614/, https://doi.org/10.17795/ijpbs-1582. Accessed 13 July 2022.

Gaur, Piyush. "The Role of Emotional Intelligence in Conflict Resolution: How to Manage Conflicts Effectively in the Corporate World?" *Www.linkedin.com*, 20 Feb. 2023, www.linkedin.com/pulse/role-emotional-intelligence-conflict-resolution-how-manage-gaur. Accessed 16 July 2024.

Gottman, John. "Emotional Intelligence Creates Loving and Supportive Parenting." *The Gottman Institute*, 8 Aug. 2018, www.gottman.com/blog/emotional-intelligence-creates-loving-supportive-parenting/. Accessed 26 Dec. 2023.

Guendelman, Simón, et al. "Mindfulness and Emotion Regulation: Insights from Neurobiological, Psychological, and Clinical Studies." *Frontiers in Psychology*, vol. 8, no. 8, 6 Mar. 2017, www.ncbi.nlm.nih.gov/pmc/articles/PMC5337506/, https://doi.org/10.3389/fpsyg.2017.00220. Accessed 9 May 2023.

He, Li, et al. "Examining Brain Structures Associated with Emotional Intelligence and the Mediated Effect on Trait Creativity in Young Adults." *Frontiers in Psychology*, vol. 9, 15 June 2018, www.ncbi.nlm.nih.gov/pmc/articles/PMC6014059/, https://doi.org/10.3389/fpsyg.2018.00925. Accessed 27 Mar. 2024.

Holland, Kimberly. "Positive Self-Talk: Benefits and Techniques." *Healthline*, 27 June 2020, www.healthline.com/health/positive-self-talk. Accessed 21 Oct. 2024.

Jardine, Brittany B., et al. "Emotional Intelligence and Romantic Relationship Satisfaction: A Systematic Review and Meta-Analysis." *Personality and Individual Differences*, vol. 196, 24 Aug. 2023, p. 111713, https://doi.org/10.1016/j.paid.2022.111713.

Jiménez-Picón, Nerea, et al. "The Relationship between Mindfulness and Emotional Intelligence as a Protective Factor for Healthcare Professionals: Systematic Review." *International Journal of Environmental Research and Public Health*, vol. 18, no. 10, 20 May 2021, p. 5491, www.ncbi.nlm.nih.gov/pmc/articles/PMC8161054/, https://doi.org/10.3390/ijerph18105491. Accessed 22 Sept. 2022.

Kim, Junhyung, et al. "The Effects of Positive or Negative Self-Talk on the Alteration of Brain Functional Connectivity by Performing Cognitive Tasks." *Scientific Reports*, vol. 11, no. 1, 21 July 2021, www.nature.com/articles/s41598-021-94328-9, https://doi.org/10.1038/s41598-021-94328-9. Accessed 1 Dec. 2022.

Kitsios, Fotis, et al. "Emotional Intelligence with the Gender Perspective in Health Organizations Managers." *Heliyon*, vol. 8, no. 11, Nov. 2022, p. e11488, https://doi.org/10.1016/j.heliyon.2022.e11488.

Koubova, Veronika, and Aaron A. Buchko. "Life-Work Balance: Emotional Intelligence as a Crucial Component of Achieving Both Personal Life and Work Performance." *Management Research Review*, vol. 36, no. 7, 14 June 2013, pp. 700–719, www.emerald.com/insight/content/doi/10.1108/mrr-05-2012-0115/full/html, https://doi.org/10.1108/mrr-05-2012-0115. Accessed 14 Apr. 2024.

Lisitsa, Ellie . "Manage Conflict: Identifying Your Triggers." *The Gottman Institute*, 17 Jan. 2013, www.gottman.com/blog/manage-conflict-triggers/. Accessed 15 Jan. 2024.

Mayo clinic. "Stress Management Stress Relief." *Mayo Clinic*, 2017, www.mayoclinic.org/healthy-lifestyle/stress-management/basics/stress-relief/hlv-20049495. Accessed 12 May 2022.

Mayo Clinic . "Being Assertive: Reduce Stress, Communicate Better." *Mayo Clinic*, 29 May 2020, www.mayoclinic.org/healthy-lifestyle/stress-management/in-depth/assertive/art-20044644. Accessed 15 Mar. 2022.

Mayo Clinic Staff. "Mindfulness Exercises." *Mayo Clinic*, 11 Oct. 2022, www.mayoclinic.org/healthy-lifestyle/consumer-health/in-depth/mindfulness-exercises/art-20046356. Accessed 18 Sept. 2023.

---. "Positive Thinking: Stop Negative Self-Talk to Reduce Stress." *Mayo Clinic*, 2023, www.mayoclinic.org/healthy-lifestyle/stress-management/in-depth/positive-thinking/art-20043950. Accessed 13 May 2024.

Porter, Jane. "How Google and Others Help Employees Burn off Stress in Unique Ways." *Fast Company*, Fast Company, 16 Nov. 2015, www.fastcompany.com/3053048/how-google-and-other-companies-help-employees-burn-off-stress-in-unique-ways. Accessed 1 Dec. 2024.

Reddy, Sravani. "Grief and Emotional Intelligence: Navigating the Depths of Loss." *Medium*, 21 Nov. 2023, medium.com/@drsravanireddyg/grief-and-emotional-intelligence-navigating-the-depths-of-loss-1053f72100bb. Accessed 13 May 2024.

Resilient Educator. "Daniel Goleman's Emotional Intelligence Theory: Explanation and Examples | Resilient Educator." *ResilientEducator.com*, 2013, resilienteducator.com/classroom-resources/daniel-golemans-emotional-intelligence-theory-explained/.

S., Lata. "LinkedIn." *Linkedin.com*, 9 Oct. 2023, www.linkedin.com/pulse/enhancing-emotional-intelligence-remote-teams-case-lata-singh-dasila. Accessed 8 Aug. 2024.

Segal, Jeanne , et al. "Improving Emotional Intelligence (EQ)." *HelpGuide*, 5 Feb. 2024, www.helpguide.org/articles/mental-health/emotional-intelligence-eq.htm. Accessed 8 Mar. 2024.

Yamani, Nikoo, et al. "The Relationship between Emotional Intelligence and Job Stress in the Faculty of Medicine in Isfahan University of Medical Sciences." *Journal of Advances in Medical Education & Professionalism*, vol. 2, no. 1, 2014, pp. 20–6, www.ncbi.nlm.nih.gov/pmc/articles/PMC4235538/. Accessed 13 Feb. 2024.